From the first hoot to the ~~~~~, this here's hillbilly humor at its finest...

Farm boy Bert moved from Newton County, Arkansas to Enid, Oklahoma to live with kinfolks. Every morning he walked down to the service station to talk with folks stopping for gas. One morning, a farmer received back some change for his purchase and laid a nickel and a dime on the counter. Looking at Bert, he said. "Pick either coin you want and it's yours." Bert grabbed the nickel.

Word got around fast and more people began putting down nickels and dimes and asking Bert to choose. He picked the nickel every time, giving everyone a good laugh.

One day after Bill had picked up a bunch of nickels, the station operator said, "Bert, you sure are dumb. Don't you know the dime is worth twice as much as the nickel?"

"Oh, shore, I know that."

"Wal, why do ya keep pickin' up nickels?"

"Cuz, if I ever took a dime, they'd never give me another nickel."

~~~~~~

Billy was sitting under an apple tree reading his Bible when a smart-alecky tourist walked up.

"You believe every word in that old book?" the tourist asked.

Billy looked up and grinned, "Yep, I shore do."

"You mean you believe that Jonah was swallowed by a big fish and then coughed up on the land?"

"Shore. Ain't that what the Bible says?"

"Can you explain in scientific terms how it happened?"

"Nope, but when I get to heaven, I'll ask ole Jonah."

"Suppose Jonah isn't in heaven?"

"Then you kin ask 'em," Billy said.

Way Back in the "Korn" Fields

Dedicated to Dr. Paul Brown, a man who truly appreciates my sense of humor.

Way Back in the Korn Fields

ABSENT-MINDEDNESS

1   Uncle Leroy had such a bad taste in his mouth that he made an appointment to see his doctor. The doctor listened to his heartbeat, then asked him to stick out his tongue. "Nothing wrong," the doctor said, "except you've got a postage stamp on your tongue."

"Oh, that's whar hit is," Uncle Leroy said. "I've been lookin' fur hit fur a week."

---

2   Professor Bardwell was attending the annual faculty dinner and was seated near the president of the college. The president looked down the table and said, "Professor, please pass the nuts."

Bardwell gulped. "If you say so, sir, but frankly, some of those students don't deserve a grade."

ACCIDENTS

3   A farmer was in court testifying against a motorist who had hit his horse-drawn wagon.

The defendant's lawyer held up his hand. "Now Jethro you've done changed your story. You said at the accident scene that you warn't hurt. Now you say you were. Why did you tell my client that you weren't hurt?"

"Well, hyar's whut happened, Mr. Lawyer. Yer man's car knocked me and ma horse in a ditch. My pore ole horse was on his back, laigs kickin' in the air. I was on ma back, ma laigs in the air. Yer feller goes over and says, 'This horse is hurt,' and pulls out a gun and shoots him dead. Then he turnt to me and says, 'Now, how about you — air ye hurt?' "

ADVICE

4   A mountain preacher was quizzing his son, Abe, on the Bible. "Son, why did God make man before womern?"

The boy happened to remember a conversation between his pa and ma that morning. "I reckon, Pa," he said, "that hit was 'cause the Lord didn't want any advice on how to make man."

***

5   President Abraham Lincoln was always besieged by would-be advice givers. Everyone seemed to have the best solution for ending the War Between the States. When a delegation of congressmen came with a suggestion that appeared ridiculous to Lincoln, the President responded with this story:

A man entered a darkened theater and put his new stove-pipe hat on the next seat. A very large lady pushed in front of him and plopped down on the hat.

"Madam," said the man whose hat she had crushed, "I could have told you that my hat wouldn't fit you before you tried it on."

AGING

6   Three wrinkled-faced, ancient-looking codgers were being interviewed on a courthouse bench by a reporter for a feature in the county paper. The newspaper man asked the first, "Jeb, what do you do for fun and how old are you?"

Jeb answered, "I play checkers and ah'll be 91 ma next birthday."

To the same question, the second old man replied, "I pitch horseshoes and jist turned 95."

And the third replied, "I drink three pints of moonshine whiskey a day, smoke two cans of Prince Albert terbaccer and stay out all night whoopin' it up."

The reporter wrote this in his notebook, then said to the third man. "You didn't tell me how old you are."

"Ah was 27 my last birthday."

7   A reporter for the county newspaper interviewed for a feature the oldest man in the county. "Don't you just hate to be a hundred and one?" he asked Uncle Billy.

"Nope. Don't bother me a'tall. If I warn't a hundert and one, I wouldn't be hyar."

8   Grandpa Willie rocked by the fire while Grandma and her woman friends quilted in the back of the room. Friendly chatter, prefaced by "girl" this and "girl" that floated in and out of his hearing. Finally he rose, turned around, and addressed the gabby quilters. "Iffen you women air girls," he said, "I ain't been born yit."

9   The parents of little Betsy Miller had never bothered to apply for a birth certificate. Betsy returned from her first day of school in tears.

"Mama," she wailed, "Teacher says I ain't got no proof that I'm me."

"W'al," her mother said. "I'll jist have to write out on a tablet paper yer name, the name of me and yer daddy and the name uf the midwife who birthed ye."

The mother gave the paper to Betsy the next morning. When Betsy got there she found the paper missing. "Oh, Miss Jennie," she wailed to the teacher. "I've done lost ma reason fer bein' born."

10   Old Herbert Thompson had been before the judge five times during the last three years for stealing hogs. This time the judge sentenced

him to 20 years in the state penitentiary, with no provision for parole.

"But, Yer Honor," Herbert pleaded, "Ah'll never live long enuf to do 20 years."

"We won't hold your age against you," the judge replied. "Just do the best you can."

11   On one of their rare trips to the city, Grandpa and Grandma were intrigued by the elevators in the new bank building. Standing in front of one, they watched an old lady, bent and wrinkled, enter. They saw a light flash and she was gone. Moments later they watched amazed as the same door opened and out stepped a beautiful and sprightly young woman. Grandpa grabbed Grandma's arm. "C'mon, woman, git in thar fast. That thang will make ya young again."

12   A reporter interviewed Grandpa Jed on his 108th birthday. "Tell me, sir, to what do you attribute your long life span?"

Grandpa snapped back, "Wal, fer starters, I was born a long time ago."

13   Young Jeb had come from the city to visit his relatives. One afternoon he took a walk up the road and met his Uncle Jed.

"How's life treating you, Uncle Jed?" the city boy asked.

"Not well, not well atall. Hit's a miserable life growing old alone," Jed said.

"Nobody told me that Aunt Susie had died."

"Oh, she hain't dead. Hit's jist that she ain't celebrated a birthday in 25 years."

ANCESTRY

14   Uncle Harry and his new wife, Isobel, a native of Massachusetts, were visiting his people in Arkansas. Isobel was trying to impress the country ladies at a quilting party.

"My family's ancestry is quite old and distinguished," she intoned. "We've traced our forbears back to King John of England."

She turned to Aunt Becky, who had never been further away than Memphis, and asked condescendingly. "How old is your family, dear?"

"I cain't really say fer sure," Aunt Becky said. "All of our family records were lost in Noah's flood."

----

15   A large imposing woman, prominent in social circles, came to Abraham Lincoln asking that the President appoint her son a colonel in the Federal Army. "Mr. President," she said, "I request it not as a favor, but as a right." Then she began recounting heroic deeds from members of her family.

"My grandfather fought for the Revolution at Lexington. My uncle was the only man who didn't run away at the battle of Baldensburg. My father contended bravely at New Orleans, and my dear husband was killed in the war with Mexico."

When she paused, Lincoln spoke softly. "Madam, it appears your family has done enough for their country. Let us give somebody else a chance."

---

16   A Texas woman was talking on the phone to a friend in Arkansas. "I've been working on my family tree. but it ended up costing me more than I expected, you know."

"Oh, how's that?" said the country woman.

"I spent five thousand dollars to have them looked up."

"Oh."

"Then I spent six thousand to have them shut up."

ANGELS

17   "Pa," a little girl asked. "Why don't angels have whiskers?"

"Daughter," said the father. "I reckon it's 'cause they got to heaven by a close shave."

ANIMALS

18   "Name an animal that has legs and can't walk, eyes and can't see, a mouth and can't talk, but can jump as high as Round Top Mountain."

Nobody at the party could.

"It's a wooden horse. It's got feet and can't walk, eyes..."

"Yeah, we know," Farmer Bill said, "But how can it jump as high as Round Top Mountain?"

"Round Top Mountain can't jump."

---

19   A farmer's wife went to town to look at refrigerators. She opened the door of one and saw a rabbit inside.

"What are you doin' here?" she asked.

"Ain't this a Westinghouse?" replied the rabbit.

The woman looked at the label on the door. "Yes."

"Well, I'm westing."

---

20 Two rabbits were whispering in a briar patch just after a narrow escape from a hungry hound dog. "What a life!" moaned one.

"You said it," said the other. "You can be hare today and gone tomorrow."

---

21 Little Artie was visiting Uncle Jess in the city. "I need to earn some money," Artie said.

"Do you have a skill, son?"

"Daddy says I'm good with dawgs."

"Well, we'll put an ad in the paper that says, 'Boy experienced with dogs. Twenty-five cents to walk a little dog around the block. Fifty cents for a big dog. A dollar for a big Great Dane.'"

"That's chargin' too much for the Great Dane," Artie said. "I'll take the big dog for a dime."

"Why so cheap for a Great Dane?" Uncle Jess asked.

"I don't walk big dogs," Artie said. "I ride 'em."

---

22 Ten-year-old Jenny was taking a vacation with her Aunt Minnie who lived in St. Louis.

One day they went to the zoo. A smart alecky woman saw Jenny eying a giraffe and asked, "Hey, little girl, what's worse than a giraffe with a sore throat?"

Jenny pointed to a larger animal and chirped, "An elephant with a bloody nose."

AUTHORS

23 Samantha's fourth-grade class at Bald Mountain School was having a lesson in creative writing. "Don't copy what other people write," the teacher said. "Just be yourself and write what's in you."

Samantha wrote: "In me there's my belly, my heart, two lungs, a bunch of ribs, an apple from Grandpa's orchard, a piece of Mama's peach pie from my dinner bucket and a big wad of Dubble Bubble chewing gum which I just swallowed."

AUTOS

24 Jed Miller, Henry Hudson, Jack Johnson and Harpy Jones arrived with their Model-A pickups in a cloud of dust at Sugar Loaf Junction at the same time. Their "oogah, oogah's" were drowned out by a clap of thunder. The four Model-As ran into each other and two flipped over. Corn flew in every direction.

Bill Harper came riding up on a horse and hollered, "Anybody killed?"

"Not yet," Jed replied. "Jist give us a little time."

25 Back when the first Model T made its way into the hills, Old Custer and his son were working their corn patch when they heard an awful noise coming up the road along the creek. "Jumpin' frog skins!" said the boy. "Whatta ya think it be, Pa?"

"I don't know," Custer said, "but I'm a goin' to git my muzzle loader."

The old man ran to the fence row and got his gun. When he saw the Model T Ford coming toward him, he fired away. The driver slammed on his brakes, jumped out, and ran for his life.

Custer put the gun back and returned to the corn patch. "Didja kill the varmit, Pa?" the boy asked.

"Nope," grumbled Custer. "Shore wish't ah had. But I did make the varmint turn loose of the feller he'd swallered."

BABIES

26 Preacher Smith took a long look at the wrinkled face of his newborn son as the country doctor stood by beaming. "What are you and the missus gonna name this young'un?" the doc asked.

Preacher Smith began thumbing through his Bible and stopped at the first verse in the Book of Acts. "Theophilus, Doc. We're namin' him Theophilus."

"Why in the world do you want to give him such a name as that?"

"Cuz he's the ophilest lookin' baby I ever saw."

27   One little ear of corn asked another little ear, "Where'd we come from?"

"The stalk brought us," replied the other ear.

28   Willie and Janie became concerned that their baby boy never spoke. The child didn't say a word until he was six. Then one day at the table, the little boy said plain as anything, "Pass the taters."

Willie and Jane were flabbergasted. Willie said, "You ain't spoke before. Why didja wait 'til now?"

"Didn't need anything until now," the child said.

29   A traveling salesman found a bachelor farmer milking his one cow. "Be through in a minute," the bachelor grunted.

He finished his milking, lifted the pail to his mouth, drank deeply, poured the remaining milk on the ground and hung up the pail.

"Now," he said, breathing a sigh of accomplishment. "Milkin's over, supper's done and the dishes are put away. What do you want?"

BACKWOODSMEN

30   Two absent-minded hillbilly brothers were building a new outhouse. Lem had a hammer and one nail. He placed the nailhead against a plank and started hammering. When he saw the nail wasn't going in, he said, "Bubba, they done gone and made this nail wrong. They put the point at the wrong end."

Clem took the nail and fingered it. "Don't blame the people who made this nail, Lem. This nail is all right. Hit goes in on the tuther side of the wall."

31   An old hillbilly and his son were rocking in front of the fire on a draggy day. After a while, the father drawled, "Son, walk outside and see if it's rainin'. That way, I won't hafta worry about plowin' today"

The boy never looked up. "Be much simpler, Pa, if we jist called Ole Rover in to see if'un he's wet."

32   A mountaineer was in the big city for the first time and hoofed his way across the deep carpet of a hotel lobby. As he was struggling to scrawl his name in the register, the clerk noticed that the new guest had left a trail of mud from the door to the desk. "You could have wiped the mud off your shoes before coming into this fine hotel," the clerk said acidly.

The hill man finished writing his name and looked up in surprise. "Whut shoes?"

33   A government poverty worker was conducting a class for rural Ozark natives who had recently moved to Springfield, MO. "Now, let's talk about something with which you are all familiar," he said. "We get fur from bears. True or false?"

"True," said an old mountaineer. "We git as fur away from bears as possible."

34 Two tough old hillbillies never wore shoes. One day they were standing around the embers of a dying campfire. One said, "Lem, better move yer foot. Ya've stepped on a live coal."

"Which foot is it?" Lem asked.

35 Back during the early days of U.S. involvement in World War II, Cousin Zeke was drafted. Catching a whiff of Zeke's odor, the induction officer ordered him to take a bath. However, it took a while to undress him. When they got down to his long underwear, they discovered underneath a red shirt. "W'al, ain't this my lucky day!" said Zeke. "I've been lookin' fer that shirt fer three years."

BALDNESS

36 Preacher Dan was waxing eloquent about Heaven. "It's a bright and shining place, and there'll be no parting there."

Old Micah rubbed a hand over his baldness. "Jist lack my head."

BANKING

37   Bertie Higgins inherited some shares of stock from her great Aunt Sally in Kansas City. Bertie went to the county seat bank for advice on selling the shares. "Do you want conversion or redemption?" the bank officer said.

Bertie put on her eye glasses and looked around. "Are you some kind of preacher?"

"Well, it all depends on whether you're saving money or souls," said the banker.

---

38   A tourist stopped a small boy on the street of a county seat town. "Boy, will you direct me to the bank?"

"I'll direct ya fer a dollar," the boy said.

"A dollar! That's high pay in a little berg like this, isn't it?"

"Sure," the boy said, "bank directors are in the upper bracket."

BAPTISTS

39   A Quaker farmer was milking his cow one day when the cow kicked over the milk bucket. Patiently, the Quaker started again, but the cow kicked it over a second time. After the cow did this seven times, the Quaker walked around in front of his animal and said, "Thou knowest that I am a peaceful man and will not smite or hurt thee, but I warn thee if thou dost kick over the bucket again, I will trade thee off to a Baptist."

BARBERS

40 A tourist stopped at a barber shop in a little town to get his hair cut. When the barber began clipping, a huge St. Bernard dog got up from a corner and began walking round and round the chair. "Your dog must enjoy watching you cut hair," the customer said weakly.

"Yeah," the barber said. "Sometimes I snip off a bit of a feller's ear and he gets a tidbit."

<hr>

41 The county seat barber took a long look at young Jed's greased-down hair and asked, "Do ya want it cut, or jist the oil changed?"

BASEBALL

42 Pigeon Creek and Crossroads were embroiled in their annual baseball game. Uncle Jake, from Lonesome Valley, was serving as umpire.

The teams were tied in the third inning when Pigeon Creek's Daniel Sexton hit a long, fly ball that was blown far to the right by a wind gust and came down in a persimmon tree, sending a shower of persimmons to the ground. Uncle Jake, the ump, hollered, "Foul!"

Aunt Bessie from Crossroads screamed back. "That thar ball wuz inside the line. It was a home run and you know it, ump. You mistook it fer a big 'simmon."

Uncle Jake hollered back: "I kin tell the difference between a 'simmon and a baseball."

The two kept arguing. Finally, Aunt Bessie said, "Ump, if you were my husband, I'd p'ison ye."

Uncle Jake glared back. "Yep, and if you war ma ole lady, I'd take the p'ison."

<hr/>

43   Billy's city cousin, Henry, took him to his first professional baseball game. Billy pointed behind home plate and asked Henry, "Why does that feller in the blue suit wear that funny thingamajig over his face?"

"That keeps him from biting the players," replied Henry. "He's the umpire and likes to chew them out."

BEES

44   After they had been robbed of all their honey by the farmer, a hive of bees decided to declare war. They organized fighter squadrons and armed them with vitamin pills which they had stolen from the farmer's medicine cabinet. As their top flyer zoomed off for the first attack, the commander buzzed proudly, "There goes Vitamin Bee One!"

BIBLE RIDDLES

45   "Who came out ahead, Jonah or the whale?" Preacher Phil asked and then gave the answer: "The whale. He got all the prophet (profit)."

<hr/>

46   Billy was sitting under an apple tree reading his Bible when a smart-alecky tourist walked up.

"You believe every word in that old book?" the tourist asked.

Billy looked up and grinned, "Yep. I shore do."

"You mean you believe that Jonah was swallowed by a big fish and then coughed up on the land?"

"Shore. Ain't that what the Bible says?"

"Can you explain in scientific terms how it happened?"

"Nope, but when I get to heaven, I'll ask ole Jonah."

"Suppose Jonah isn't in heaven?"

"Then you kin ask 'em," Billy said.

47   A bunch of fishermen were telling stories. "Boys," said one, "did you hear what the big shark said when he heard the whale talking about how he had swallowed a bunch of people?

"The shark said, 'I don't believe these man-stories of yours.'

" 'They're all true,' the whale said. 'You should have seen the one that got away.' "

48   Teacher: "What does the story of Jonah and the big fish teach us?"

Jerry: "You can't keep a good man down."

49   Jed: "Who suffered most when the prodigal son returned home?"

Ned: "I know. The calf. His fat was in the fire."

50   The history teacher asked little Jethro, "Who was Joan of Arc?"

Jethro grinned back. "I know. She was ole Noah's wife."

51   Preacher Phil stopped for a pastoral visit with Uncle John and Aunt Minnie. After a few moments of conversation, he mentioned that he would like to read a passage of Scripture and pray before leaving. "I don't have my Bible with me," he added. "May I use yours?"

About that time, John and Minnie's granddaughter came in the house. "Sweetheart," Aunt Minnie said, "would you go into our bedroom and bring Brother Phil the book we love so much."

A moment later the granddaughter returned with a mail order catalog.

52   A man who lived far back in the sticks desired to enter the ministry and went to a bishop of his denomination to be examined. The following conversation took place:

"Can you read, Jethro?"

"Naw, sah, I cain't read a lick."

"Can you write?"

"Nope. Cain't write either, but ma old lady is a pretty good scribbler."

"Well, do you know your Bible, Jethro?"

"Yep. I'm purty smart in the Scriptures. I know the Good Book from lid to lid."

"Which part of the Bible do you like best?"

After thinking a minute, Jethro replied. "I reckon, the Book of Mark."

"What passage in Mark do you like best?"

"I reckon that'd be the parables."

"And which parable is your favorite, Jethro?"

"W'al, bishop, I kinda favor the Good Samaritan. I lack that 'un the best."

"Very good. Now can you recite the parable of the Good Samaritan?"

"Yes, sir. Ah will, sir. Hyar goes:

"Once thar was this feller walkin' from Jerusalem to Jericho, and he fell among thorns, and them thorns sprung up and choked his gullet. An' as he journeyed on, he didn't have no money, and he met that thar Queen of Sheba, and she give him a thousand talents of gold and a hundert changes of raiment. An' he jumped in a chariot and drove like a scalded dawg, and when he was drivin' under a big jumper tree, his hair caught on a big limb, and he hung thar many days, and some ravens brought him some grub to eat and some water to drink. He et 5,000 loaves of bread and two big fishes — I think they war catfish. So's one night while he was a hangin' thar a snorin' in his sleep, his wife Delilah come along and clipped off his hair, and he drapped down on stony ground. But he got up and moseyed on, and hit begun to rain, an' hit rained forty days and forty nights, an' he hid hisself in a cave, and he lived on locusts and wil' honey.

"Yuh want me to go on, bishop?"

"Finish, Jethro. I've never heard a parable recited like that."

"W'al, bishop, he went along down the road, 'til he met up with a sharecropper, who said,'Come, take supper at ma house.' An' he excused hisself and said, 'I cain't go today. I've married a wife, an' jist cain't git away.' An' that sharecropper went out in them highways and hedges an' made him come in.

"So's after supper, he come on down to Jericho. An' when he got thar, he saw ole Zaacheus settin' high in a tree. ' Zaacheus,' he said to the man, 'Go on down to the barn 'an see ol' Queen Jezebel settin' high up in the loft.' An' when he got thar and seed the queen, she haw-hawed at him. An' he said, 'Pitch her down out uf that loft!' And they throwed her down. An' he said,'Throw her down agin.' An' they throwed her down seventy times seven, an' uf the pieces, that remained, they picked up twelve baskets full, not countin' the womern and chillern. An' they said,'Blessed air the piecemakers.' Now, bishop, I ask ye, whose wife do ye thank she'll be in the Jedgement Day?"

53 Billy was asked by his Sunday school teacher to name his favorite parable. "I like that one where ever'body loafs and fishes," he replied.

54 Jeb was intrigued with the speaker system at the county fair. "Do you know who invented the first loud speaker?" he asked his pal, Joey.

"Nope," Joey said. "You tell me."

"The Lord made the first loud speaker from Adam's ribs."

"Sure enough," replied Joey. "An' ah bet ole Adam tuk an awful ribbin' fur it."

BIBLE

55   When was the longest day in Bible times? *When there was no Eve.*

56   How do we know Adam and Eve were rowdy? *They raised a little Cain.*

57   What is the strongest day in the week? *Sunday. The rest are "week" days.*

58   Who was the Bible's best doctor? *Job. He had more "patience" than others.*

59   Who got the most applause in the Bible? *Samson. He brought down the house.*

60   What Bible character slept in a crowded bed? *Moses. He slept with his forefathers.*

61   How many pieces of forbidden fruit were eaten in the Garden of Eden? *Eleven. Eve ate (8); Adam, too; (2) Satan won (1).*

~~~~~~

62   When was the first baseball game in the Bible? *Genesis 1:1. "In the big-inning."*

~~~~~~

63   Why couldn't Noah play cards? *Because Mrs. Noah sat on the deck.*

~~~~~~

64   Why was Noah unprepared to go fishing? *He had only two worms and had to save them.*

BIRDS

65   The Washington Biological Survey wrapped some metal bands on legs of wild birds to chart their migratory habits. The bands carried the simple abbreviation: "Wash. Biol. Surv." Several months after the birds were released, a hunter downed one in Arkansas. The Ozark mountain man wrote, "Dear guver'ment: I shot one of yer birds and did what you wrote on its leg. I warshed it. I b'iled it. I surved it. It tasted orful. Who air you tryin' to fool?"

BOREDOM

66   Alexander Woollcot knew how to handle a bore. Once when he thought that a monologue of an acquaintance had gone on too long, Woollcott interrupted. "Excuse me, my leg has gone to sleep. Do you mind if I join it?"

BOOKS

67 A class in Mountain Top High School was asked to list new inventions they would most like to see. Sweet Susie wrote: "A perfumed bookmark. If it slipped down into the book, you could just sniff along the edge 'til you found your place."

68 Uncle Ben spent every Saturday curled up with a horror novel. One day a neighbor asked Aunt Jenny what Ben did for exercise.

"Oh, he reads and let's his flesh creep," she said.

69 Jimmy John had been married six months when he went looking for a book in the county seat library. "Do you have a book on how to understand women?" he asked nervously.

"The fiction shelf is on your right," she said.

BOSSES

70 After high school graduation Geraldine moved to Kansas City and got a job as a secretary in a large office. One day the big boss was busy and asked her to check the employees' suggestion box. When she came back, he asked her what was in the box.

"I can't figure out what lake and kite they're talking about," she said.

71 "Didja ask the boss for a raise?" Julie

asked her friend, Janice who had just come out of the big office.

"Yes," said Janice, "and he was a perfect lamb as I had figured."

"For true? What did he say?"

"Bah!"

---

72   The price of hogs was good that year and Bill bought his wife, Mabel, a piano. A couple of weeks later her boss at the courthouse, where she was a secretary, dropped by for a visit. Mabel offered to play a few tunes she had learned.

As she was thumping out a melody, Bill leaned over and whispered to her boss, "With three children, Mabel doesn't get to play as much as she'd like."

The boss whispered back, "Aren't kids a blessin'."

BOY SCOUTS

73   A Boy Scout chapter was finally organized in Deer Creek township. At the second meeting, the scoutmaster asked, "Did any of you boys do any good deeds today?"

Five hands shot high in the air. Buster spoke for the lot. "All of us carried Aunt Susie across the road this morning?"

"Why five?" the scoutmaster asked?"

Buster: "She didn't want to go."

---

74   The town of Edgarville was staging a

mock tornado. The Boy Scouts were assigned to act as injured persons to be discovered and tended to by the Girl Scouts. But the girls got so far behind schedule that one Boy Scout gave up after waiting for his rescuers for over an hour. When the girls finally arrived at his spot, they found a note that said, "I bled to death and went home."

BREVITY

75 Among all U.S.presidents, Calvin Coolidge was most known for his brevity. This was well illustrated on the occasion when his former classmate asked him to send a cable message collect to be read at their class reunion. The cable was received by one of the group and given to the master of ceremonies at the reunion dinner. At the appropriate time, the emcee rose to announce that a message had come from their most famous classmate, the President of the United States.

The applause was deafening. The guests pushed their chairs around and looked expectantly to the speaker's table. The emcee unfolded the cablegram and read this message:

"Greetings. Calvin Coolidge."

BUGS

76 The boys and girls in Professor Madison's biology class decided to play a joke on their teacher. They caught a butterfly, a grasshopper, a centipede, a bedbug and a wasp, and glued various parts of the insects' bodies together, making a strange composite creature which they placed on Dr. Madison's lectern.

The professor saw their creature immediately. "Where did you catch this strange specimen?" he asked in pretended curiosity.

"We caught it in the weeds near the football field," they said. "We thought you might be able to tell us what it is."

The professor placed the bug under a magnifying class and examined it top, bottom and on all sides. Finally he looked up and smiled slightly. "Was it humming when you caught it?"

"Yes," they answered in chorus.

"Then," said the professor, "I pronounce this creature a humbug!"

BUMS

77   A shiftless man knocked on the door of a farmhouse and asked for something to eat. "Before I give you a sandwich," Grandma said, "let me show you something." She took the bum out to the backyard and showed him a pile of logs. "These logs need cutting for our fireplace. Do you see them?"

"Yep, I see 'em."

"You should say, 'I saw them.' "

The bum looked at grandma. "Ma'am, you saw me see 'em, but you ain't gonna see me saw 'em."

78   Panhandler: "Mister, will ya give me five dollars for a cup of coffee?"

Well-dressed man: "That's too much for one cup of coffee, isn't it?"

Panhandler: "Well, yes, but I'm puttin' all my

begs in one askit."

<hr>

79   Back in the 1940s a group of hoboes were talking under a new overpass as streams of cars rolled overhead. It was the Saturday before the Fourth of July. "Holidays make me feel awful ordinary," said one. "All them people goin' on picnics and camp-outs. Ain't nobody workin'."

BUSES

80   Aunt Sarah took the Greyhound bus from Kansas City, Missouri to see her sister in St. Louis. At the bus station she hailed a taxi and asked the driver to let her off on Lindbergh Boulevard, two blocks from her sister's house. "I don't want Sis to hear the car stop," she said. "I want to slip up and surprise her."

Aunt Sarah became real anxious when they got in her sister's part of town. She'd never been in St. Louis before. Every hundred yards or so, she kept reminding the driver to drop her off on the boulevard two blocks from her sister's house. Finally, she said, "How will I know you're dropping me off at the right place?"

"By the smile on my face, madam," said the annoyed driver.

<hr>

81   Tom, a country boy with long legs and big feet, was taking his first bus ride. He hadn't been told that he should stand up and give up his seat if a lady walked on. The bus stopped and picked up an older woman who shuffled over near him, expecting him to courteously stand up. When he didn't move, she put her full weight down on one of his feet.

"Excuse me, lady," Tom said, "but I think you're standin' on my feet."

"Oh, am I?" the old woman replied. "If you were a gentleman you'd be standing on them yourself."

82   A missionary was driving a small tour bus loaded with visiting pastors from America. Several miles out in the jungle they came upon a sign: "CANNIBAL VILLAGE, 50 MILES AHEAD." Driving on, they came to a cluster of thatch huts and read another sign: "TAKE THE BUS AND LEAVE THE DRIVER TO US."

BUSINESS

83   A tourist in Maude's Cafe complained that his breakfast sausages looked funny with meat at one end and bread crumbs at the other.

"I have to fix the sausages that way to stay in business," Maude said. "In these times of rising costs, nobody can make both ends meat."

84   A butcher was brought to court for selling horse meat. "It warn't all horse meat, Your Honor," he pleaded. "Jist half and half."

"What do you mean?" the judge asked.

"Half horse and half chicken."

"How many chickens to the horse?"

"Why, one chicken to one horse," said the

butcher.

---

85 George Miller ran the country store on the corner. His third cousin, Bill Johnson, ran the other store in town. "There ain't nuthin' I wouldn't do fer Cousin Bill," said George, "and there ain't nuthin' he wouldn't do fer me. That's the way we are. We go through life doing nuthin' fer each other."

---

86 Farm boy Bert moved from Newton County, Arkansas to Enid, Oklahoma to live with kinfolks. Every morning he walked down to the service station to talk with folks stopping for gas. One morning, a farmer received back some change for his purchase and laid a nickel and a dime on the counter. Looking at Bert, he said. "Pick either coin you want and it's yours." Bert grabbed the nickel.

Word got around fast and more people began putting down nickels and dimes and asking Bert to choose. He picked the nickel every time, giving everyone a good laugh.

One day after Bill had picked up a bunch of nickels, the station operator said, "Bert, you sure are dumb. Don't you know the dime is worth twice as much as the nickel?"

"Oh, shore, I know that."

"Wal, why do ya keep pickin' up nickels?"

"Cuz, if I ever took a dime, they'd never give me another nickel."

CANNIBALS

87 Two cannibals, a father and son, were walking across an open field. Suddenly a small, single-engine plane roared overhead and the son grasped his father's leg in fright.

"No need of bein' scared, son," the big savage said. "It's only an airplane."

"What's that?" asked the trembling boy.

"It's sort of like an ocean crab, son. The outside's tough, but the insides are delicious."

---

88 The new missionary came into his house after teaching his first day of school in a cannibal village. "How did things go today," his wife asked.

"Not so good. I had to expel two kids. They tried to butter up the teacher."

---

89 A U.S. Peace Corps worker was sent to a cannibal tribe. When the man was not heard from, his supervisor sent a message by jungle runner to the cannibal chief, asking about the man's welfare.

The chief patted his stomach. "Him good, very fine. We'd like another taste of democracy."

---

90 An American soldier was on a Pacific island and met a native carrying a Bible. "When you get educated," the soldier said, "you'll find that book won't be necessary."

The native smiled back and patted his stomach. "Well, it's good for you that I'm not educated yet. Or else you'd be in here by now."

CATHOLICS

91 Two Catholic monks set up a fish 'n chips stand in front of the rural monastery during the tourist season. Soon a woman came along and asked, "Which one of you is the fish fryer?"

One monk pointed to the other and replied, "He is, ma'am. I'm the chip monk.

CATS

92 A cat sat on a fence watching a tennis game. Another cat jumped up and said, "You act like a real tennis fan."

"No," I don't really care for the game. I'm just here because my daddy's in the racket."

93 "Mr. Bolin, do you know the difference between a cat and a comma?" asked smart-aleck Johnny at Red Rover School.

The teacher reckoned that he didn't.

"W'al, a cat has claws at the end of its paws. A comma's a pause at the end of clause."

CEMETERIES

94 What did one casket say to another?

"Is that you, coughin'?"

95 An Ozark boy took a shortcut through a graveyard one dark night and accidentally fell into a freshly dug grave. He tried several times to climb out, but finally gave up and sat down in a corner to wait for morning. He was dozing off to sleep when another youth came along and fell in. Unaware of the first boy's presence, this second boy began trying to climb out.

Wide awake now, the first boy reached over and tapped the newcomer on the shoulder. "Might as well keep me company. I couldn't git out either."

But the second boy did!

CHEERLEADERS

96 A girl studying to be a cheerleader took a course called Rah-Rah 202. When the teacher began lecturing about "Tah-Ra-Boom-De-A," the girls asked, "Isn't this Rah-Rah 202?"

"No." the teacher replied. "That's a course of a different holler."

CHILDREN

97 Trailed by his baby brother, the little hillbilly boy edged up to the tourist. "Mister, give us a dime and my little brother here will make like a hen."

"I don't like to hear a boy cackle," the tourist said.

"Naw, nothin' lack that. That's baby stuff. Little brother will swaller a worm."

---

98 Two country kids walked into a country store. "Gimme a dime's worth of them jelly beans on that top shelf," one said.

Uncle Harry, the aging grocer, carefully climbed up on his step ladder. Before coming down he asked the second boy, "Do you want the same, son?"

"Nope," the boy said.

Uncle Harry climbed down. "What do you want then?"

The boy replied with a straight face. "Only a nickel's worth. That's all the money ma would give me."

---

99 Traffic was at a complete standstill. Little Willie and his daddy got out of their truck and joined the crowd that was watching a large house trailer stuck halfway under a railroad overpass. Men were feverishly trying to push the trailer through. Finally Willie walked up and pulled on one of the men's pants leg. "Mister, why don'tcha try lettin' some air out of the tires?"

It worked.

---

100 Little Susie and her parents were on vacation in the Ozark mountains. Susie saw her first snake.

"Come quick, mommy," she squealed."Here's a tail wagging without a dog."

---

101 Teacher: "Children, make a sentence using the word, 'gruesome.' "

Little Mary: "Daddy shaved because he gruesome whiskers."

102 Little Jiminy came home on the school bus with a swollen and very black eye. He was watching the TV news, when his mother came in and asked what had happened.

"Oh, nothing much, Mother. I was hit by a guided muscle."

103 Spoiled Billy had seldom left his mama's side during all his five years. But finally he parted from her and climbed on the school bus to attend his first day of kindergarten.

His mama worried about his welfare until he came home. When he finally arrived, she grabbed him up and held him tight. "Did you cry, Little Darlin'?"

"Nope," the spoiled kindergartner said. "But Teacher did."

104 Margie Johnson had to take her two pre-school children with her to church where she was to attend a meeting of the kitchen committee. She left the kids in their Sunday school room to play while she met with the adults in a room nearby where she could hear her little ones talking.

The meeting was well underway, when Margie lifted a hand. "Shhh," she said. "Listen and you'll hear my two darlings saying their prayers."

The ladies stopped and listened reverently. They heard a squeal: "Mama, Willie found a roach and is eatin' it!"

***

105 Lenny was forever asking questions at the country school. Finally his weary teacher said, "Curiosity once killed a cat. Don't ask so many questions."

Lenny thought about this for a long time, then asked, "Teacher what did the kitty want to know?"

***

106 Eleven-year-old Jeri Lynn told her girl friend, "If I ever stop hatin' boys, Jake will be the one I stop hatin' first."

***

107 Worried mama: "Doctor, how is my dear little boy — you know, the one that swallowed a quarter this mornin'?"

Doctor: "No change yet."

***

108 First-grade girl to her teacher: "If I sit across the aisle from Billy, does that mean I'm the opposite sex?"

***

109 Two eight-year-old cousins were talking about what time they had to go to bed. "I have to go to bed at eight," Mary said. "My mamma is an hour meaner than yours."

***

110 A mother came home from shopping at

the county seat and asked her seven-year-old Minnie who had stayed home, "What all did you do while Mommy was gone?"

"I was a helper, Mommy. I took some letters over to the postoffice and asked Uncle Jack to put one in every box."

"Oh, and where did you get all the letters?" the mama asked with a gnawing fear.

"I found them in your bottom dresser drawer all tied up in a blue ribbon."

111 One day Abraham Lincoln was strolling along a street in Springfield, Illinois with his two boys. Both were unhappy and wailing loudly.

"Mr. Lincoln, what's the matter with your boys?" asked a passerby.

"Just what's the matter with the rest of the world," Lincoln replied. "I've got three walnuts and each boy wants two."

CHINESE

112 An exchange student from China came to live with a farm family way back in the hills of southern Missouri. The host father began proudly showing off the family's modern conveniences. He picked up a telephone book. "We can find in here the number to call of every family in the county."

The Chinese youth courteously nodded, pretending to be impressed.

"I don't suppose you have telephone books in China," the farmer said.

"Oh, we have them, but we don't let visitors

from America use them."

"Why not?" the farmer asked indignantly.

"A thousand pardons, honorable sir, but we have so many Wings and Wongs, we're afraid that our guests will wing the wong number."

CHURCH ATTENDANCE

113 Many years ago, an elderly lady visitor from Little Rock, Arkansas brought her ear trumpet to church in rural Madison County. Deacon Jud, a native of Scotland who didn't trust city folks anyway, tapped her on the shoulder. "I'm a warnin' you, woman. One toot and you're oot."

CHURCH BUSINESS MEETINGS

114 "How was your church business meeting last night?" the Methodist preacher asked his Baptist counterpart when they met at the cafe for their usual morning cup of coffee.

"It was like a cold," said the Baptist. "They went back and forth on giving me a raise in salary. Sometimes the eyes (I's) had it and sometimes the nose (No's)."

CHURCH CHOIRS

115 The Crossroads Church choir was practicing a new anthem. "Now remember," the director drawled., "the sopranos will sing until we get to the River Jordan. Then the rest of you will come in."

116 Grandpa Mose's hearing aid batteries gave out in the middle of the first line of the choir anthem. He didn't hear a word from then on.

After the service, Grandpa grabbed Doc Hughes, the town physician who was also a deacon in the church. "I heard the choir singin', 'Ever' Christian ought to take a pill...a pill.' Then my batteries bopped out. What kinda pill war they singin' about, Doc?"

Doc had to shout in Grandpa's ears to be heard. "A pilgrimage, Grandpa. Every Christian oughta take a pil-grimage..."

CHURCH DENOMINATIONS

117 Little Nathan came with his parents from Missouri to visit their kinspeople in Ohio. After dinner, Nathan and his cousin, Sally, went outside. "Let's play church," Nathan suggested.

"Okay," said Sally, "but first I've gotta ask Mama."

A minute later Sally came back shaking her head. "Mama says we can't play church 'cause we belong to different abominations."

CHURCH MEMBERS

118 Pastor John was discouraged with the non-attendance of so many members. He began checking the roll and calling upon those he had never seen in services.

One man he visited acted very nasty. "Preacher, the church has done nothing but

disturb my life," he said. "First, they put water
on me. Second, they tied me to a woman I've had
to support ever since."

"I understand," interrupted Pastor John,
"and the next time you come, they'll throw dirt
on you."

119 A church and a honkytonk were located
on the highway, only a quarter mile apart. The
manager of the honkytonk had a trained parrot
that told saucy jokes to the customers. The
parrot had a nest in the joint's loft and came out
when called upon to entertain.

One Saturday night the honkytonk burned
and the parrot flew away to a place of safety.
Noticing that the church had a high ceiling the
bird found a roosting place on a huge beam that
hung directly over the pulpit.

On Sunday morning the parrot was
awakened by a crowd of people coming into
service. He looked straight down at the pastor
behind the pulpit and chirped, "H'mmmm, got a
new manager of the joint." Then he saw the choir
file in and said, "H'mmmm, got some new
singers, and they've got clothes on, too." Then
he swiveled his head to survey the congregation.
"Hey, I'm beginning to feel at home now. There's
some of my same old crowd."

120 Two maiden ladies were on their way
home from church.

"There were so few at church today," said
one, "that when the minister said, 'dearly

beloved,' I thought he was proposing to one of us."

~~~~~~

121   An elderly rural preacher was once asked how many active members he had in his church.

"They're all active," he said. "Half of them are working with me and half are working against me."

~~~~~~

122   A note in a church bulletin announced the reorganization of the Brotherhood: "Starting next Monday night the men of the church will reform."

CHURCH MUSIC

123   Uncle Harry, a deacon in a small country church, went to Denver to visit his children and attended church in their impressive new sanctuary. When he got home he tried to tell his neighbor about the fine anthems he had heard.

"What's an anthem?" asked the neighbor.

"Well, now, it's like this. If I told my wife, Matilda, 'I want apple pie,' that wouldn't be an anthem. But if I hollered, 'Mah-til-ldah, Mah-til-lllldah, Mah-tlllll-dah, I your husband, I your husband, I your husband, yes, I your husband, yes, I your husband, want, want, want, want, yes, I surely, surely do want apple pie, app-app-apple pieeeeee. Ah-h-h-h-h — men-n-n-n-n-n,' then that would be an anthem."

CHURCH OFFERINGS

124 His first time in church, little Jeremy watched the ushers collecting the offering. When the plate started along his pew, Jeremy squeaked loud enough for all to hear, "Don't put in fer me, Pa, I' ain't yet six."

125 A father wanted to develop his son's character and gave him a nickel and a silver dollar as they were entering the church. "Put one in the collection plate," he told his son.

After church, he asked the boy which coin he had given. "I pitched in the nickel, pa. Jist 'fore they passed the plates, the preacher said, 'The Lord loves a cheerful giver.' I figured I could be more cheerful if I gave the nickel, so that's what I did."

126 A preacher's son applied to become a county deputy. During his exam, the sheriff asked him, "How would you scatter a crowd?"

Quickly, he replied, "I'd take off my hat and start takin' up a collection."

127 The community tightwad shook hands with the minister at the end of the service. "Fine sermon. I ain't got nuthin' but praise fer you and this church."

"So I noticed when the offering plate was passed," thought the minister.

128 An itinerant preacher delivered a sermon and then passed a hat around a county fair crowd to pay his travel expenses. After a long time the hat came back with only a few nickels and dimes. He shook out the few coins, then raised his eyes upward and prayed, "I thank Thee, Lord, that I got back my hat from these folks."

129 An Internal Revenue Bureau agent telephoned a Baptist preacher and said, "I'm going over the tax return of one of your church members, a Mr._____. He lists a donation of $960 to the church. Can you tell me if he made this contribution?"

The preacher replied, "Well, I don't have the financial records before me — but if he didn't, he will!"

130 As old Joe lay dying he told his wife, "Elizabeth, look in my little black book and you'll find where Jack Brown owes me $500, Bill Henderson owes me $600 and my nephew, John owes me $150."

The wife turned to her children and dabbed at her eyes. "You see what a wonderful man your father was. Always helping people."

"And I want you to remember," Joe continued, "that we are behind on our church pledge $400."

"Ha, ha," his wife laughed. "Children, your

father's goin' out of his mind again."

CHURCH SERVICES

131 A woman complained to a church usher. "Somebody is occupewing my pie."

"I'm sorry, sister," the usher replied, "I'll sew you to another sheet."

---

132 Four-year-old Brenda was attending the "big people's church" for the first time. Her older brother, Jim, gave her some last minute instructions.

"Remember now," he said, "they don't 'low you to talk in church."

"Who don't 'low you?" she asked.

"The hushers. That's who."

---

133 Teacher: "Jerry, describe hibernation for the class."

Jerry: "Hibernation is a state of stupor which some animals enter in winter. It is a kind of suspended animation during which the animal seems barely alive."

Teacher: "Very good. Now can you give us an example?"

Jerry: "Yeah, like my father in church."

---

134 On a trip to Little Rock, Uncle Orvil walked into a dignified worship service in a very formal church of his denomination. He sat down in a pew near the front. The minister had just started his sermon, when Uncle Orvil said fervently, "Amen!"

An usher across the aisle frowned. The people around the visitor cleared their throats.

A few minutes later, Uncle Orvil said a little louder, "Praise the Lord!"

The usher glared at him this time and the entire first and second rows frowned.

A little later, Uncle Orvil shouted, "Well, praise God. Ain't it wonderful!"

This time the usher leaned across the aisle and whispered, "Please control yourself sir. We don't do that here."

"But I've got religion," Uncle Orvil explained.

"Well, you didn't get it here," the usher growled back.

CHURCH STAFF

135 When Pleasant Woods Church bought a new organ, they also hired a janitor. Before, volunteers had been cleaning the church. The janitor was an elderly man who had a natural gift for music. He got the organist's job too.

A few weeks later, a visitor to the church asked him how he managed to do both jobs so well.

"I mind my keys and pews," he said.

CHURCH USHERS

136 A small dog was chased out of the church at Four Corners by a near-sighted usher. Aunt Jenny arrived late and entered the church with the pesky dog trailing at her heels. This time the usher grabbed a broom and followed Aunt Jenny and the dog down the aisle. His aim was poor, and he hit Aunt Jenny on her heels.

"I'm really sorry I'm late," Aunt Jenny said. "I had trouble startin' my old car."

137 A Methodist pastor invited three Baptist preacher friends to attend the dedication of his church's new building. However, the Baptists arrived late and all the pews were filled. A hard-of-hearing usher took the three visiting preachers down front and looked at his pastor for instructions.

"Glad to have my Baptist brethren with us for today's dedication," the Methodist preacher said as he looked at the usher "Get three chairs for them, Brother Bill."

The hard-of-hearing usher looked puzzled, but dutifully turned around to face the people and said quite loudly, "Okay, folks, our pastor says give three cheers for the Baptists — hip, hip, hoorah!"

CIRCUS

138 Reb Hill made his living with a circus. When this circus folded, Reb asked a friend with another circus to recommend him for a job. The friend pumped up Reb's qualifications to the circus manager: "You oughta see ole Reb put his right arm into a lion's mouth."

The manager was impressed. "Tell him to come down and talk to me. By the way, what's his name?"

"Lefty," replied the friend.

COACHES

139 Coach Johnny Winner was real anxious for a country boy athlete to be accepted by the college. So the coach set up an interview between the boy and the dean, and went along to give the prospective football player some support.

"I'll just ask you a simple question," said the dean, "and if you can answer it, we'll give you a football scholarship. How much is six plus six?"

The boy thought a while and answered, "Thirteen."

A long silence followed. Finally the coach said, "Aw, Dean, let 'em in. He only missed it by two."

COBBLERS

140 A country boy came into a shoe cobbler's shop and asked, "What do you use to fix shoes?"

"Hide," the cobbler said.

"What?"

"Hide, hide — the cow's outside!"

The boy exclaimed, "Shucks, I ain't afeard uf no ole cow."

COFFEE

141 Recipe for hillbilly coffee: Take two pounds of coffee, wet it down with cold branch water, bile over a hot far fer an hour, pitch a choppin' ax in it; if the ax sinks, throw in another pound of coffee.

COLLEGES AND UNIVERSITIES

142 A proud young man marched into the personnel office of a large company that had located in a rural area. "Here I am with an A.B.," he announced.

"Fine," said the personnel secretary, "Now sit down and ah'll teach you the rest of the alphabet."

143 "What happened to Susie," a coed asked her friend. "Why did she drop out of college?"

"Haven't you heard?" the friend replied. "She got married and retired from the human chase."

144 "What is your son at the university?" the county agent asked the farmer.

"He's a fullback," the farmer said proudly.

"No, I'm talking about scholastic rank?"

"Oh, in grades, he's away back."

145 A college boy sent a telegram home, saying, "Mom, have failed everything. I'm coming home. Prepare Dad."

The boy received this reply the next day: "Dad prepared. Prepare yourself."

146 An unambitious country bumpkin went to college and on his way into the administration building was asked by another student, "What are you going in for this semester?"

"Because it looks like rain," he said.

147 One farmer to another: "What's your son taking at college?"

"Every dime I've got," was the reply.

148 Clem and Mary came to town to see their daughter graduate from college. Walking into the auditorium for the ceremony, they heard people around them extolling the accomplishments of their children.

"My son is graduating summa cum laude," said one.

"My daughter is graduating magna cum laude," said another. This parent looked at Clem and Mary, "I suppose you've come to see your child graduate."

"Yep," said Clem proudly. "And our daughter is graduating magna cum laundry. She worked her way through school in the washateria.

COUNTRY

149 The country boy thought a long time about the question on his college exam in his physical education class: "How may one gain good posture?"

Finally he wrote, "Keep the cows off it and let it grow awhile."

150 Country music's Grandpa Jones tells about the "good ole days" when he performed way back in the mountains of West Virginia. On one occasion he was invited to perform for a family get-together. Following directions, he turned off the main highway on to a dirt road. The road ended in a creek bed. He followed the creek bed three or four miles and turned right on an old wagon road. At the end of the wagon road, he came upon a log cabin. When nobody came out in response to his holler, Grandpa walked over to the door and found a note that said, "Gone to the country."

COMMUNISM (SEE ALSO SOCIALISM)

151 One day in school a Cuban boy was asked, "Who were the first human beings?"

"Adam and Eve," the boy answered.

"And what nationality were they?"

"Cuban," the boy replied.

"You're making progress," the teacher said. "How do you know they were Cuban?"

"That's simple. They had no roof over their heads; they didn't have any clothes to wear; they had only one apple between them; and they called it paradise!"

152 Before Communism collapsed, the former Soviet Union gave millions of rubles to keep Fidel Castro's Cuban economy running. One year both the Soviet and Cuban economy were bad. Castro telegraphed Moscow: PLEASE SEND FOOD, COMRADES.

The Kremlin wired back: TIGHTEN BELT, COMRADE.

Castro wired again: PLEASE SEND BELT.

153 In the old days, before communism fell in the Soviet Union, a Russian wolfhound visited Paris and became acquainted with a French Poodle. "Life is great under communism," said the wolfhound. "Because I belong to the Party I've got an air-conditioned doghouse, plenty of juicy meat and all the rabbits I want to chase."

"Whatever made you come to Paris, then?" asked the poodle."

"I felt an overpowering urge to bark for a few days."

154 Back when communism ruled in Eastern Europe, a manager held a weekly meeting of his workers on a collective farm. After the manager had bored the workers with his standard lecture on the advantages of communism over capitalism, a girl named Marie asked, "Sir, if our system is so good, why must our country import food when under capitalism we exported a surplus?"

The manager did not blink as he said, "I'll study that situation and report back next week."

The next week the manager gave his usual lecture and then asked for questions. After a pause, someone asked, "Where's Marie?"

COMPUTERS

155 A tired looking man dragged himself through the front door and slumped into a chair.

"Hard day at the office, dear?" his wife asked sympathetically.

"Awful," he sighed. "Our computer link broke down in the middle of the afternoon and we all had to think for two hours."

CONFESSIONS

156 A French count and an accomplisce stole the queen's jewels. The king forced the count to confess, but the count wouldn't tell who helped him. Finally the king handed down an ultimatum to the count: "Tell or be beheaded."

Still no word came from the count. As the count was being led to the chopping block, he was offered another chance to tell. Again he refused. Then as they started down, the count yelled, "I'll tell! I'll tell!" But the axe fell and his cry was too late.

Moral: "Don't hatch your counts before they chicken."

CONSERVATION

157 A conservation officer from Little Rock was talking to an Ozark audience about protecting national forests. "Has someone here contributed something to conserving our timber resources?" he asked.

When no hands were raised, Tim, a well known hunter spoke up. "Well, sir, I once shot a woodpecker."

CONVENTIONS

158 For their accomplishments in farming,

Lem, Hank and Joe were given a trip to a growers convention by a private foundation. They were given a room together on the 75th floor of a hotel. After the first session of the convention, Joe left their keys with the desk clerk. They went out and walked around and didn't return until about two a.m. When they shuffled into the lobby, the clerk told them the elevators had broken down and they would have to walk up the 75 flights of stairs.

The three men started for their rooms. Halfway up the first flight of stairs, Lem suggested they do something to keep their minds off the long climb. "I'll sing country songs, the first 25 floors," Lem said. "Hank, you tell country jokes the next 25, and Joe, you tell sad stories for the last 25."

The other two agreed and Lem sang until they reached the 26th floor, then Hank told jokes. When they came to the 51st floor, Joe stopped and didn't say anything, Lem said, "Okay, you can start your sad stories."

"I'll tell the saddest one first," Joe said. "I just remembered that I forgot to get the room keys."

COUNTERFEITERS

159 A slick confidence man was handed a roll of $18 bills by a counterfeiter. "The machine got mixed up," the counterfeiter said. "We can't use these in the big city. Take them down to the Ozarks and pass them off to the hicks."

The con man took a bundle and drove deep into Newton County, Arkansas. He stopped at a crossroads store, asked for a candy bar and a soda pop, then handed the storekeeper one of the crisp $18 bills. The storekeeper took it without blinking and said, "How'd you like yer change? A nine and an eight er two sixes and two threes?"

COURT

160 Judge to lazy moonshiner: "Have you ever been up before me?"

Moonshiner: "Can't remember if I have, Your Honor. What time does your rooster crow?"

161 Three boys were hauled into county juvenile court. "Name and offense," the judge asked the first boy.

"Jim Smith and I've been throwing peanuts into Bull Shoals Lake."

The second said, "Bill Brown and I've been doin' the same."

The third one said, "Peanuts."

COURTSHIP

162 Sarah Ann was calling her old high school chum, Maggie, who had stayed in the hills to be near her boy friend. "Any hint of marriage yet?" she asked.

The stay-at-home girl replied, "I've made at least a dozen, but so far he just ignores them."

163 Shy Pelly brought his girl, Rosie a bouquet of wild flowers, whereupon she suddenly threw her arms around him and kissed him. When Pelly started backing up, she blushed and said, "I didn't mean to be so forward."

"I'm not complainin'. I'm jist goin' to get more flowers."

∙∙∙

164 Billy Ray, a high school boy, was saying for the 20th time to his girl, Cherry at midnight, "How can I ever leave you?"

Cherry's father growled from the stairs, "If your car won't start, I'll take you home."

my father once told me to tell a boyfriend "Here's your hat, what's your hurry"!

165 Jerry to his new girl friend: "Since I met you, darlin', I can't eat, I can't sleep, I can't drink."

"Why not?"

" 'Cause I'm broke."

∙∙∙

166 Jim Bob wrote this rhyme to let his girl know that he was running short of money:
"Twas in a restaurant they first met,
Romeo and Juliet.
Twas there that he got into debt,
Cause Rom-e-owed what Juli-et."

∙∙∙

167 Cynthia to pesky Harold: "What's the difference between a car, a sigh and a monkey?"

Pesky Harold to Cynthia: "I dunno."

Cynthia to pesky Harold: "The first is so dear, the second is, 'Oh, dear,' and the third is you, dear."

168 "Will you love me when I'm gray?"
Said the young girl to her steady.
"Yes, I'm sure I will," he said.
"I've loved a dozen shades already."

169 A bored Velma rocked indifferently on the porch swing with the ardent Cameron. A harvest moon was casting pale golden light over the rippling waters of the nearby farm pond. When Velma stopped talking, Cameron leaned close and whispered in her ear, "Say those three little words that'll have me walking on air."

Velma could stand it no longer. She jumped off the swing, whirled around to face Cameron, and said, "Go hang yourself!"

170 When the young newly engaged couple returned home from their date, the girl's younger brother was sitting up reading. "Guess what, Bill? Your sister and I are going to be married," said the young man to his future brother-in-law.

"You just findin' that out?" said the unimpressed little brother.

171 Sixteen-year-old Betsy smiled when the bell rang. "Answer the door and let him in," she called to her younger brother.

The younger brother went to the door and called back upstairs. "Sorry, but that wasn't the dreamboat you were lookin' for. It was just the old tub from down the road."

―――――――

172 "Face powder will land a man," said the young girl as she applied makeup before her mirror.

"Yes," said her older sister, "but bakin' powder will keep him."

―――――――

173 A farmhand asked his employer for a lantern to carry on a "courting" visit. "Young feller," the farmer said, "I can't figure why you need a light to go sparkin'. In my time we never used a lantern for that."

"And look what you got," said the farmhand.

―――――――

174 Oswald to Bobbie Sue: "If ya don't say ya'll marry me, I'll jump off that cliff down thar."

Bobbie Sue: "Os, I don't believe you. That's only a bluff."

―――――――

175 Troy and his girl, Billie, were madly in love and talking about marriage when Troy moved to Joplin, Misssouri and took a temporary job, where he hoped to save up enough money to buy Billie an engagement ring. To maintain his devotion, he sent her a letter every day for the next three months. At the end of the three months, he got a letter from Jenny saying she was marrying the mailman.

176 Bachelor Buster fell deeply in love with a young mountain school teacher named Helen. For her birthday, he wrote a note saying he was going to send her a rose for each year of her life.

He picked 29 roses from his mother's garden while his nephew, little Eddie, an admiring student of Helen's, watched. After Buster wrapped the roses in a pillow case, Eddie sneaked in a dozen more because he liked the teacher so much.

Poor Buster never did know why Helen turned down his marriage proposal.

177 Teacher to Billy Bob: "Why do bees buzz?"

Billy Bob: "You'd buzz too if somebody took yer honey and nect-'ar."

178 LeRoy was telling his pal, Hobert, about his first visit to an amusement park. "I went into the Tunnel of Love and it was pitch dark...."

Hobert: "Did you have a girl with you?"

LeRoy: "What fer? Mama taught me not to be scared of the dark."

179 "Sue," said ardent Jimmy Jack, "I shore am carryin' a torch fer ya."

"How couldja?" she replied indifferently. "You ain't that bright."

COWS

180 A city girl made her first visit to the farm where her boyfriend was working during the summer. As she watched a cow chewing its cud, her boyfriend remarked, "Nice looking cow, don'tcha think?"

"Yes," the girl agreed, "but the farmer must have a big chewing gum bill."

CREDITORS

181 Billy Bob bought a car on credit. Three months later his timber cutting job ran out and he couldn't make the loan payments. He drove to St. Louis to see his cousin, Jerry, and look for another job. On Saturday, Jerry took him to the aquarium where Billy Buck became captivated by an octopus.

"Kin you loan me a little money?" he asked Jerry.

"What for?"

"I wanna buy that octopus and put the squeeze on the loan company for a change."

CULTURE

182 An artistically minded girl married a country boy and brought him to the city. One day she dragged him to an art museum. As they entered she said, "I'm so excited. There's a Rembrandt on display."

The country boy looked at the door leading into the museum and mumbled, "Now how in the world did they ever manage to get a sports car through there?"

CUSTOMERS

183 At the crossroads store, Arnold picked out four red apples and handed the storekeeper a dollar. The merchant gave him back a penny in change.

Arnold pushed the penny back. "You keep it, Horace. I stepped on a grape on the way in."

DEACONS

184 Back in the 1930s, a small, southern mountain church was having a business meeting. After all the usual stuff was cared for, the preacher asked if anyone had anything special to say.

Deacon George stood up and said, "I think we need a chandelier for the church."

Whereupon Deacon John objected.

"Why don't you think we need a chandelier, Brother John?" the preacher asked.

"Well, first, nobody in the church can spell it; second, nobody in the church can play it; and third, what this church needs more than anything else, is more light!"

DEFENDANTS

185 "Now, Joe," the judge said to Round Mountain's most shiftless character, "Do you solemnly swear to tell the truth, the whole truth, and nothing but the truth?"

Joe nodded and lifted his hand.

"Let us hear what you have to say in your defense."

"Wal, Yer Honor," replied Joe, "with the

limitations ya put on me, I don't reckon I've got anythang to say."

DENTISTS

186 An old codger went to the dentist in the county seat back in the 1930s to have a bad tooth pulled. When the job was done, the dentist handed him a bill for $6.

"Six dollars, Doc, is a lot of money for the five minutes you spent pullin' that tooth," the codger protested.

The dentist grinned. "Well, if you think so, I'll pull the next one slower."

187 Centerville got a lady dentist. Her first patient was Uncle Willie who told her, "I've been looking forward to this visit."

"Oh," she said, "do you have a toothache?"

"Not that I know of. I just come to hear a woman say, 'Open your mouth,' instead of, 'Shed up!'"

188 A dentist was being sworn in as a witness in a county seat trial. The county judge leaned down and asked, "Do you promise to tell the tooth, the whole tooth, and nothing but the tooth?"

DETERMINATION

189 One cold February day a little snail started climbing an apple tree. As he inched slowly upward, a worm stuck its head from a crevice in the bark to offer some advice. "You're wasting your energy, snail. There isn't a single apple up there."

The snail kept up his slow climb. "There will be when I get there," he said."

DINNERS

190 Uncle Ben was invited to a fancy Thanksgiving dinner at his brother's house. His seat was near the head of the table where the host was carving the goose. "Ah," Ben exclaimed, "You've put me next to the goose."

Noticed the cold look of the woman on his right, he corrected himself quickly."The roasted goose…"

~~~~~~

191 A country Methodist preacher was invited to a ministerial association dinner in Fort Smith, Arkansas. He found himself seated beside the visiting Episcopal bishop who was to address the group. Ill at ease, yet determined to put forth his best manners, the rural parson said, "May I pass you some grace, Your Gravy?"

DISCIPLINE OF CHILDREN

192 Little Rudy hadn't behaved too well in church while the pastor was preaching on the 23rd Psalm. As a punishment, his mother set up a small table near the large dining table and told him he would have to eat alone. After all of the kinfolks were seated for Sunday dinner, Rudy's father started to give thanks. But his prayer was broken up by Rudy who was heard to say,

"Thank you, Lord, for preparin' a table 'fore me in the presence of my enemies."

※※※※※※※※※※※※※※※※※※※※※※※※※※※※※※※※※※

193 Little Johnny misbehaved and his mama told him to go and sit on the back porch until his daddy came home to give him a spanking. Instead, he ran in his room and crawled under the bed.

His daddy finally arrived and was told Johnny had a spanking coming. He looked on the back porch and not finding Johnny there, went to the boy's room and peeked under the bed.

"Hi, Pa," Johnny whispered. "Is she after you, too?"

DISTURBANCES

194 Mark Twain was just starting a lecture when the steam pipes in the old building began making an unearthly racket. Every time Twain started to say something, the pipes hissed and banged. Finally, he shouted above the clamor, "Will somebody go down in the cellar and tell that janitor to stop gnashing his teeth?"

DIVORCE

195 Back in the 1940's a divorce was rare in Ozark communities. Naturally, news of a split-up would cause a lot of talk. In one instance, two women were discussing the report that one of their cousins and his wife were getting a divorce. Said one of the women: "I thought they were a perfect match."

"Yes, they seemed to be," said the other who had lived in California awhile. "But you never know how the tied will turn."

---

196 A woman whose last name was Coffeepot came to court seeking a divorce. The judge refused because she had no grounds.

DOCTORS

197 Ole Doc Bristow was trying to diagnose the toughest case he had ever seen in his country practice. For an hour he searched his medical school notes and books. Finally he walked back to see his patient. "Aunt Minnie, have you ever had this trouble before?" he asked.

Aunt Minnie nodded. "Last year I had an attack."

"Well," said the doc, "you've just had another one."

---

198 Farmer Brown came stumbling into Doc Holloway's office saying he was losing his eyesight. Doc restored his sight, but erased his memory. When Doc brought back his memory, Farmer Brown's eyes clouded over again. Finally, Doc asked him which he would prefer, his eyesight or his memory. Farmer Brown replied, "I'd rather see where I'm goin' than know where I've been."

199 Doctor to country boy: "Son, you have acute appendicitis."

Country boy: "Thank ye kindly, Doc, but I come here to be examined, not bragged about."

200 Cousin Goober swallowed a quarter. When the coin didn't pass, he went to the doctor. Upon returning home, he told his mama, "Now I know what a specialist is. He's a fancy doctor who can take a feller who has swallered a quarter and make him cough up $25."

201 The trembling farmer opened the door wide to admit the young doctor. "She's upstairs, first room on the right," he said. "You go see what's ailin' her while I wait down here. I always was a little skittish of any sickness."

The young doctor, fresh out of his internship, hurried up the rickety stairs. A moment later he yelled down, "Get me a screw driver." The farmer obediently complied.

Another minute later, the medic hollered, "Get me a hammer." Puzzled, but still trusting the young doctor, the farmer handed up a hammer.

But when the doctor called for a chisel, the farmer could trust him no longer. "What's wrong with her, doc?"

Back came an apologetic answer. "Don't know yet. Still trying to get my bag open."

202 Absent-minded doctor to wife: "Now why did you tear out a bunch of pages from my new medical book?"

Wife: "Excuse me, dear. I guess I copied your habit. That part was titled 'Appendix' and I took it out without thinking."

203 The doctor was greeted apologetically as he entered the farmhouse at a late hour. "I'm terrible sorry to ask you to come out on a snowy night like this," the wife said, "but Bill is really in pain."

"Quite all right, Sally," the doctor said. I have another patient out this way, so I can kill two birds with one stone."

204 The excited wife called the doctor in town. "Hurry to our house on MacArthur Mountain, Doctor. My Willie is at death's door!"

"I'll be there in half an hour, Audrey," the doctor replied, "and pull him through."

DOGS

205 Said one flea to another as they came out of a restaurant, "Shall we walk or take a dog."

206 The county game warden stopped by the Brown's farmhouse and saw their little boy, Benny, playing in the yard. "Hey, son, do all your daddy's dogs have licenses?"

"Shore do. He's out back tryin' to get rid of 'em with lye and hot water."

207 What did the Indian say when his dog fell from the cliff?"

"Dog gone!"

208 A skunk family was hemmed in by a pack of hound dogs. As the hunters and dogs moved near, the mother skunk said to her brood, "Children, let us spray."

DRIVERS

209 Remember the Burma-Shave highway slogans?
   They Missed
   The Turn
   Car Was Whizz'n
   Fault Was Her'n
   Funeral His'n
   Burma-Shave

210 Sign at entrance to a trailer park in a wooded area of the south: DRIVE SLOW. OUR SQUIRRELS DON'T KNOW ONE NUT FROM ANOTHER.

211 A state patrolman noticed a car weaving from side to side and stopped the young bimbo driver. When he asked for her license, she giggled, "What a silly question, officer. Now, who do you think would give me a license?"

***

212 A wise guy stopped on an Montana highway where a woman was standing beside her upside down car. "Did you have a wreck?" he asked.

"No," she replied. "I turned it upside down to change a tire."

***

213 A country woman drove a pickup truck into Nashville for the first time. She stopped for a red light and became very tense at the sight of a long line of cars whizzing down the cross street. When the light turned green, she did not move, fearful it would change color before she could cross. The light changed colors several more times and still she did not move. Finally a policeman walked over and said, "Lady, don't we have any colors you like?"

***

214 Roscoe Smith was stopped by a patrolman. "Young man, you were going eighty in a forty-mile zone," the cop said.

"I warn't even goin' fifty," retorted Roscoe, "nnnnor forty, nnnnnor thirty, nnnnnnor..." He suddenly noticed the cop writing a ticket. "Whut are ya chargin' me with?" he asked the officer.

"Improper backing, son. Improper backing."

215 Billy Bob returned to Arkansas after living in southern California for a couple of years. "What kinda drivers do they have in Californy?" his cousin, Joe Ben asked.

"Jist two kinds," Billy Bob replied, "and they named baseball teams after them. Dodgers and Angels. And the traffic's so bad on them freeways, you're either one er the other."

216 Sam was just home from the hospital and giving his neighbor some friendly advice. "Man, if your wife ever wants to drive, don't stand in her way."

217 A motorist walked wearily into a rural store. "How far to the nearest filling station? he asked.

"Four miles as the crow flies," the storekeeper replied.

"How far," the tired driver mumbled, "if the old crow has to walk, carryin' a gasoline can?"

"In that case," said the storekeeper, "I'd advise the crow to call the station for road service."

DRUGGISTS

218 A man raced into a drugstore and asked the pharmacist, "How do you stop the hiccups?"

The pharmacist promptly delivered a stinging slap.

"What's the big idea?" the man yelled. "I oughta —"

"You don't have the hiccups anymore, do you?"

"No," the man shouted, "but my wife out in the car still has."

DRUNKS

219 Two drunks were stumbling along a railroad track. Said one, "I don't like all these steps."

Said the other, "Whut I hate worse than the steps are these low hand rails."

220 The swine court was in session behind the barn. A young pig was before the bench charged with getting drunk the night before. He had partaken from the dregs of beer cans thrown behind the tavern.

"Do you have anything to say before I pass sentence?" the judge hog grunted.

"Your honor," the accused grunted back, "please give me a light sentence, and I'll promise never to act like a human again."

221 Two drinking friends were remembering the tragic death of a pal. "Too bad Joe got careless," said one.

"Yeah, he spilled rum on his whiskers," said the other.

"That wouldn't have killed him," said the first, "except he struck a match to light his cigar."

"And," concluded the second, "he could have lived. But he just fiddled with his whiskers while rum burned."

~~~~~~

222 A drunk picked a number at random from the telephone directory and called it at three a.m. After a few rings a sleepy voice mumbled, "Hello."

"Is Bill Smith there?" the drunk mumbled.

"Sorry, but you've got the wrong number," the man said patiently.

"Thirty minutes later the drunk called and again asked for Bill Smith. This time the man was more abrupt.

The third time the drunk called, the man slammed the phone down in disgust.

Finally, about 5:30 a.m. the drunk called once more and said, "This is Bill Smith. Any calls for me?"

EATING

223 Mother Sarah was pleading with her young son to eat all his spinach. "Come on, Johnny," she begged. "Think of all the children in poor countries overseas who would love some nice spinach like this."

Johnny looked up and demanded, "Name two."

~~~~~~

224 Skinflint Bill Campbell snapped at his wife for requesting an extra five dollars in grocery money. "Woman, whut have ya been doin' with all the grocery money I give ya?"

"Stand sideways and look in the big mirror," she replied. "You'll see."

225 Too little to save,
Too much to dump,
That's what makes
The farm wife plump.

226 A long-time acquaintance invited an old college chum to dinner on Cape Cod. When asked how the dinner went, the host said, "She ate so many clams that her stomach rose and fell with the tide."

ECONOMICS

227 Uncle Jed did some figuring. He added up all the retired people past 65, plus those under 18, plus those in hospitals, prisons and on welfare. After subtracting the total from the nation's population, he said, "There's only two left, and ah'md tard of supportin' half the country."

228 Grandpa Charley, the hillbilly economist, divides workers into two classes: "Folks who earn their livin' by the sweat of their brows, and those who sell them handkerchiefs, cold drinks and air conditioners."

EFFICIENCY

229 Granny Griddle was proud of her efficiency. She was always trying to find a better way to do something. When she died at 94, it took six pallbearers to carry her to her last resting place. As they came near the grave, the coffin lid popped open. Granny sat up and declared. "If you'uns would put wheels under this thing, you'd only need one man to pull it."

ENTERPRISE

230 Sure to make a fortune: The designer who can make a woman's shoe larger on the inside than it is on the outside.

EVOLUTION

231 Uncle Ed, a born poet, happened to catch on TV a lecture by a learned professor on the subject of evolution. When the program ended, Uncle Ed wrote a poem for the professor:
"Once I was a tadpole when I began to begin.
Then I was a frog with my tail tucked in.
Next I was a monkey on a coconut tree.
Now ah'm a doctor with a Ph.D."

EXAGGERATION

232 A country preacher was given to exaggeration in speech. Aware of this weakness, he asked his wife to shake her head when he began to stretch the facts. One morning he was telling about a tornado he had witnessed. "I saw that long black funnel cloud swoop down from the skies and clear a rightaway across the country a thousand miles long."

Suddenly he caught sight of his wife frantically shaking her head. He added, "...And an inch wide."

~~~~~~

233 Little Jerry ran into the house and said, "Mama, I saw a bug as big as a hound dog."

"Jerry," his mama scolded, "hain't ah told ya a million times not to stretch the truth."

FALLING

234 Cousin Howard led a party of tourists to the edge of a high bluff overlooking the Buffalo River in Newton County, Arkansas. One of the tourists asked, "Do people fall from here very often."

"Jist onct. Jist onct!" said Cousin Howard.

"Didn't anybody ever survive," the tourist persisted.

"One rich feller did," replied the guide. "He was a soft touch."

FAMILY

235 The first-grade teacher was getting acquainted with her pupils. "Jimmy," she asked, "Tell me about the people in your family."

"Oh, we're just one big happy bunch of animals."

"What do you mean by animals?"

"Well, Mama is papa's deer, baby is mama's little lamb, brother is jist a kid and papa's the old goat."

236 "Our new pastor talks so fast I can't understand him," said one lady.

"Blame his family," replied her husband. "His father was an auctioneer and his mama was a woman."

FARMERS

237 An easy-going farmer in Sunday school told how he applied the verse, "Take no thought for tomorrow" to his life: "When I work, I work hard; when I sit, I sit loose; when I worry, I fall asleep."

238 Two Missouri farmers had lived in the same community all their lives, but had never talked much. One afternoon they struck up a conversation. "Hey, Jeb," said one, "what did you give yer horse when he had that colic?"

"Turpentine," replied Jeb.

A month later they met again. "Did you say, Jeb, that you give yer colicky horse turpentine?"

"Shore."

"Well, I give my ole mare turpentine and she died."

"So did mine," said Jeb. "So did mine."

239 One day a rich city gambler was riding by a farm in his new sports car and saw what looked like a beautiful young race horse. Hoping to buy the horse and make a big profit, he went to the farmer and said, "I think your horse looks pretty good, so I'll give $500 for him."

"Oh, he don't look so good," the farmer said. "He's not for sale."

I can sell him for $5,000, the gambler thought. So he offered the farmer a thousand, adding, "I think your horse looks fine."

"Well, if you think so," said the farmer as he took the gambler's money.

The next day the gambler returned in a rage. "You sold me a blind horse!" he screamed.

"I know it," the farmer said calmly. "Didn't I tell ya, he don't look so good."

240 An old farmer accompanied his son on a plane trip. When the plane landed in Kansas City, a small yellow gasoline truck sped up with fuel. Later, when the plane landed in Des Moines, the same thing happened again. "This plane sure is fast," commented the son.

"Yep," the farmer said, "and that little yeller truck does pretty well, too."

241 A city man decided he wanted to be a farmer. He went to the bank to draw out his savings. "Are you sure you know what you're doing?" the banker asked. "Have you had some experience in farming?"

"Nope," said the man, "but I know how it works. You make a down payment on some land, get your implements and seed on credit, and by the time you get everything going a drouth comes along. After that, the government steps in and keeps you going."

---

242 Motto of a lady farmer: "Look like a teenager, act like a lady, think like a man, work like a dog."

---

243 They strolled down the lane together.
The sky was studded with stars.
She stood at the gate in silence,
As he lifted down the bars.
She neither smiled nor thanked him
Because she knew not how,
For he was just a farmer's boy
And she was a jersey cow.
(From *Newton County Times*)

FASHIONS

244 Store supervisor to a little lost boy: "Why didn't you hang on to your mother's skirt?"
Little lost boy: "I tried, but I couldn't reach it."

---

245 A *Newton County, Arkansas* farmer listened patiently to a young preacher give a long sermon which contained little more than stray bits of information and exhortations. It reminded the old farmer of loose hay whirling around in a high wind. At the door, when the service was over, the old farmer said, "Young feller, don't you figure it would be better to bale yer hay before you deliver it to the cattle?"

246 Sam the sage says: "The way some women dress, you can't tell whether they're inside trying to get out, or outside trying to get in."

247 Farmer Caleb's daughter, Holly, bought a pair of fashionable textured stockings. Her mother was displeased and asked Caleb, "What do you think of them?"

Caleb glanced at the new stockings. "Let it be. If it doesn't go away in a week or two, we'll call Doc Moppins."

248 Two country drunks were walking through the new shopping mall. "Whash that sign shay?" asked one.

The other, who had had less to drink, peered at the store front and said, "Ladies Ready-to-Wear Clothes."

Whereupon the first drunk shouted, "Hooray! Ish time the fashions were changin'."

FATHERHOOD

249 Father to son's teacher: "And how is my Joey doing in history? Never was good at it myself."

Teacher: "History is repeating itself, sir."

250 Two old friends were reunited after an absence of 20 years. When one learned that the other had five daughters, he remarked, "You must have a tough time keeping the wolf from the door."

"Oh, I do pretty well," he replied, "but I do have problems feeding the pack, though."

251 A farmer was scolding his teenage son for idling. "You ought to be ashamed. When President Lincoln was your age he kept busy building rail fences. You won't even do your school work."

"Yah," said the impudent boy, "and when Lincoln was your age, pa, he was President of the United States."

252 Two kids were discussing the talents of their parents. "My dad's a clerk in a country store," said one.

"That's nothin'," said the other. "My pa's a second story man."

"What's that?"

"If Mama don't believe his first story, he tells a second one."

253 Two little boys were talking about their fathers at mealtime. "What does your daddy say when your family sits down at the table?" asked one.

"He says grace," replied the other. "What does your's say?"

"My daddy says, 'Don't drink too much milk. It's gone up, you know."

FIGHTING

254 Boy (bragging to his chum): "I had a fight with Bull Taylor and when it was over, he came to me on his hands and knees."

"What did he say?"

Boy: "Come out from under that porch, you coward!"

FILMS

255 A movie company came into the Ozarks to shoot a film. After the visitors left, two goats came looking for something to eat. One goat sampled a piece of film that had been discarded. "How'd it taste?" the other asked.

"Not so good," said the first goat. "I liked the book better."

FISHING

256 A fellow from Illinois loved fishing, just loved it. One of his life-long dreams was to go fishing on Bull Shoals Lake in the Arkansas Ozarks. He'd heard many tales of the big bass that were to be found there, so finally he decided to take his yearly vacation in the Ozarks Mountains.

He got himself a motel room a few miles from the lake, and early the next morning he set out on his big adventure. Stopping at a bait store on the way, he asked the hillbilly behind the counter for a bucket of worms.

"Are the bass biting down on Bull Shoals?" he asked the hillbilly.

"Shore are," he replied in a slow drawl.

The fellow started thinking. *Maybe one bucket of worms wouldn't be enough. I'd hate to get out on the lake and hit a big pocket of fish and then run out of bait. Maybe I should consider getting two buckets.*

He called over to the hillbilly. "Maybe I should get two buckets of worms. Well, how many worms are in a bucket anyways?"

The hillbilly turned slowly towards the fellow, "Don't worry. You'll have enough. Life's just too short to be counting worms."

257 Two fishermen met on Arkansas' Buffalo River and found they were both from Chicago. "Why did you come so far?" asked one.

"I came because this is set apart as a wilderness river by the National Park Service. I wanted to tread through virgin forests, swim in crystal clear waters, and leave my footprints on clean sand beaches. Now, why did you come?"

"It's this way," replied the other. "My son got a new horn for Christmas. My daughter started taking lessons on the tuba, and my mother-in-law began using our home to record her voice on tape."

258 Two fishermen were trying to out brag one another. Said one: "Mine that got away was so big he almost flipped over the boat with his tail."

"The last one I caught didn't get away," said the other. "It was too little to truck home. Three game wardens had to help me pitch it back in."

259 A man stopped his car on a bridge and called down to the fisherman below. "Any luck?"

"Nah," the man said as he reeled in his lure. "But you should have been here yesterday. I caught six times the legal limit."

"You don't say," said the spectator. "Did you happen to know that I'm the new game warden in this county?"

"Sure enough," replied the fisherman, "and you ain't been here long enough to know that I'm the biggest liar in this county."

260 A skilled angler was hauled before the county judge by the game warden and charged with catching five times his limit of bass. "That'll be $100 plus court costs," the judge said. "The clerk will give you a receipt."

"Sure, Your Honor," the fisherman said. "And could you tell the clerk to give me six copies for my friends?"

261 Tip from Hooter Holler Guide Service to fishermen who have trouble with wives: "To keep fish from smelling, cut off noses."

262 Down on Buffalo River a fisherman noticed another man down the stream was hauling in bass hand over fist. So he moved down and began catching fish also. The other fisherman was miffed at the intrusion. He gathered up his gear and stalked away, grumbling as he walked.

A woman fishing nearby commented, "I'm glad that old grouch is gone. I hate to fish around anyone that crabby."

"Apparently he didn't like our presence," said the fisherman who had moved down. "Do you know who he is?"

"Ought to," groaned the woman. "I've been married to him for 35 years."

---

263 Orvil was the laziest fisherman who ever lived in Booger Holler. One day he was lying in the sun, rod and reel in hand, when the fisherman next to him fell in the Arkansas River. As the poor man came up for the second time, lazy Orvil said, "Next time you go down, check the bait on my hook."

FLYING

264 Many Scotch immigrated to the Ozarks during the 19th century. During the early days of aviation, a descendant of one of the old Scotch "Mc" families and his wife were watching a pilot give exhibition plane rides in a pasture alongside a creek. The Scotchman asked the cost and was told $5.00 per passenger. He waited another hour until all the other customers had left. Realizing the type of man he was dealing with, the pilot made this proposal: "I'll take you and your wife both up for nothing provided neither of you says a word. If either of you speaks, the ride will cost you $10."

The Scotchman agreed and they took off. For

a half hour the pilot dived and looped. When he finally landed, the pilot said to the Scotchman. "The ride's for nothing. I didn't hear a word from you or your wife."

The Scotchman sadly shook his head. "Thanks, but I almost talked when my wife fell out."

265 Grandpa got on the big passenger jet to take his first plane ride. When the motors roared, he gripped the arms of his seat in terror and closed his eyes. About ten minutes later he looked out the window. He turned to the man beside him. "Jist as I expected. The people down there look jist like ants."

"They are ants," the man explained. "We're still on the runway."

FOOD

266 Irvin Cobb was once dining at an inn in Pennsylvania and asked the waiter about the history of the establishment. "It's very old," said the waiter. "It goes back to the times of the American Revolution. There are many interesting stories."

"Yes, there must be," said Cobb. "Could you tell me the legend of that strange old mince pie that you just served?"

FOOTBALL

267 A skinny country boy back in the 1930s had never seen a football game. When the newly consolidated high school hired a new football coach, he applied for the most envied position on the team.

"Nope, I've already got me a quarterback," said the coach. "But I'll give you three other positions to play. You can be end, guard and tackle."

"How can I play all these positions, coach?"

"You can sit at the end of the bench, guard the water bucket and tackle anybody who comes near it that's not on our team."

---

268 The football coach was worried because his number one and number two quarterbacks had been taken out of the game with injuries. He looked down his bench of subs and yelled at his third-string quarterback, "Okay, Leroy, go in the game and get ferocious!"

Leroy leaped to his feet. "What's his number?"

---

269 Country boy Vester returned home from his first day of high school football practice. "Did you make the team?" his daddy asked eagerly.

"I'm not sure," Vester replied. "When I walked on the field, the coach said, 'This is the end.'"

---

270 An Alabama teacher asked her third grade class to make a list of the eleven greatest men in the country. Two or three minutes later a little tow-head raised his hand. "I've got nine already, teacher, but I can't decide who I want to put down as the center and right tackle."

***

271 A tight-fisted country squire spent thousands of dollars to send his son to college. In the son's senior year, the father moaned, "Look at all the money I've spent on that boy. And all we've got now is a quarterback."

***

272 A bunch of relatives were talking about the illness of rich Uncle Joe. One of them, a sports fan, noted, "Dear old Uncle Joe is like a football player and we're the people sitting in the stands, waiting for him to kickoff."

FORGETFULNESS

273 Daryl and Janie were sitting in church when Janie suddenly remarked, "Oh, how awful! I forgot to turn off the electric iron before I left the house."

"Don't worry about that, honey," Daryl said. "It won't burn long. I just remembered I forgot to turn off the faucet in the bath room."

FRIENDS AND FRIENDSHIP

274 "Long Distance calling Mr. Joe Johnson," said the operator.

"Hello, Joe," said an anxious voice. "This is your ole coon-huntin' buddy, Bill Henderson. Listen, Joe, I'm stuck here in Chicago and need $200."

"I can't hear you," said Joe. "Something must be wrong with the phone."

"I need $200," Freddy shouted.

"I still can't hear you," Joe said again.

Just then the operator interrupted. "I can hear him real plain."

"Fine," Joe said curtly. "You send him the $200." And with that Joe hung up.

---

275 Mark Twain was at a dinner party when a lady noted that he was not participating in a discussion of eternal life and future punishment. Finally she remarked, "Mr. Twain, please give us your opinion."

Twain replied gravely, "Madam, you must please excuse me. I am silent of necessity. I have friends in both places."

FUNERALS

276 A wayward fellow with little education died and the preacher was fumbling through the funeral sermon. He ended with the prayer, "And, Lord, we hope he's where we think he ain't."

FURNITURE

277 A husband grew tired of the conversation carried on between his wife and her hi-falutin' cousin. When the cousin remarked, "We have an antique sofa that goes back to King Louis the 14th," the husband broke in to say: "How nice. We have one that goes back to the finance company on the 15th, don't we, dear."

GAMBLING

278 The rain was streaming down in Las Vegas. The doorman at a gambling palace was saying, "Why walk in the rain, folks? Come inside and really get soaked."

GARBAGE

279 Garbage pickup had finally come for the folks who lived along 'Possum Road. Julie's husband had already gone to the corn field to work when she heard the garbage truck coming down the road. "Oh my, he forgot to put the garbage out when he left," she said.

Julie was still in her old floppy housecoat and her hair looked like a crow's nest. Nevertheless, she came running out with the trash. "Am I too late for the garbage?" she hollered at the driver.

The garbage man took one look and replied, "Naw, lady, jist come and jump right in."

GARDENING

280 Old Jerry, the head gardener at the big country estate, was always bragging about the importance of past jobs. One day the old gardener told a visitor, "I once worked on a place with a thousand people under me."

"Where was that?" the visitor asked.

"A fancy graveyard called Memorial Gardens."

GIFTS

281 An Arkansawyer who got rich from raising and processing chickens was always trying to outdo his wealthy Oklahoma cousin in sending gifts to their grandmother. The Arkansawyer heard about an amazing zirkah bird that could speak five languages. He found the bird and bought it for $25,000 and sent it to his grandmother for Christmas.

He called her the day after Christmas and asked, "How did you like the zirkah bird, grandmother?"

"Very appetizing," she said. "I et it before the turkey."

"Grandma, I didn't mean for you to eat it," he declared. "That bird spoke five languages."

"It did?" said the grandmother. "Then, why didn't it say something?"

GOLDEN RULE

282 The Sunday school teacher was applying the Golden Rule. "Just remember, boys and girls, that God put us here to help others."

Johnny raised his hand. "Well, then, teacher, what are the others here for?"

GOLF

283 An insurance agent and his businessman neighbor were playing golf.

The neighbor slammed the ball hard, then remarked, "Playing golf is like my business. I drive hard to get to the green, and then wind up in the hole."

284 Two golfing buddies had been searching for a golf course in the country. They left their golf clubs in their car and dropped into church, thinking somebody there could direct them to the course. The preacher was orating against evolutionists. "They'll never find the missing links," he shouted.

"Aww, and we were hoping you would tell us how to find them," one of the golfers remarked.

285 A male golfer took his wife to the course. She kept asking questions until he became thoroughly annoyed."There are enough traps on this course already," he shouted. "Please close yours while I swing."

286 Without realizing the danger, a cluster of ants built a mound near a golf tee. The next morning a golfer appeared. He missed the ball on his first swing and clipped off half of the ants. He swung again and hit the other side of the ant hill.

Only two ants were left alive. Said one to the other, "You know, if we're going to stick around, we'd better get on the ball."

287 "I reckon I'll have to wear my golf socks today," the husband grumbled as he rummaged through a dresser drawer.

"What golf socks?" she asked.

"The ones with 18 holes in them."

288 Two Mexican detectives were examining

the body of a man named Juan Martinez.

"How was he shot?" asked the first.

"I think it was with a golf gun," said the other.

"But what ees a golf gun?"

"I'm not sure, but eet sure made a hole in Juan."

GOSSIP

289 How do you make a mountain out of a molehill? Just keep adding dirt.

290 Three kinds of gossips: The collar button type — always popping off; the vacuum cleaner type — always picking up dirt; the liniment type — always rubbing it in.

291 Preacher Sam Jones said he knew a woman with a tongue so long she could sit in the parlor and lick the skillet in the kitchen.

292 Why do dogs have more friends than humans? Because the wag is in their tails instead of their tongues.

293 Gossipy woman over backyard fence: "Didja meet our new neighbor? Hasn't she got big teeth?"

"Yeah. Everybody in town knows when she uses her electric toothbrush. The lights go dim."

294 Will Rogers suggested that we should so live that we wouldn't be afraid to sell the family parrot to the town gossip.

295 Two gossipy women hadn't talked to each other for several weeks. When they met on the street, one gushed, "Oh, Jenny, let me tell you about all the things that have happened to me since we last talked. I've had all my upper teeth taken out — and a new stove and sink put in!"

296 Two gossipy ladies boarded a jet for the first time. One implored the pilot: "Please don't go faster than sound. We want to talk."

297 A man with a reputation for spreading tales came forward in church at the end of a sermon on Christian love. He told the minister, "I've come to lay my tongue on the altar."

The preacher, who knew the tale-spreader all too well, shook his head and said, "I'm afraid our altar isn't long enough for your tongue."

298 A country woman hurried across the road to see her neighbor. "It's a principle of mine never to say anything about a person unless it is something good." She paused for breath, then added, "And, girl is this good!"

GOVERNMENT

299 A husband and wife were touring the Arkansas capitol building in Little Rock. Their guide pointed to a tall, smiling gentlemen, noting that he was Chaplain of the Arkansas Legislature.

The lady asked, "What does the chaplain do? Does he pray for the Senate or House?"

The guide answered. "No, he stands up, looks at the Legislature, then prays for the state."

300 Unofficial definitions from the Washington bureaucracy:

"Program": Any job that cannot be completed by one telephone call.

"We are aware of it": We hope the goofball who started it would have forgotten by now.

"Under consideration": Never heard of it.

"Under active consideration": We are looking in the files for it.

301 An Oklahoma politician was warming up his audience and remarked, "I won't defend or criticize the state budget. It's an imaginary figure that doesn't really mean much — merely a point at which to start an argument."

302 A hard-headed businessman complained that government arbitration is like having a dispute with your wife and going to your mother-in-law for a settlement.

303 How many government workers does it take to put in a new light bulb? Three. One to hold the bulb and two to turn the ladder.

304 Uncle Jeb says, "Folks hereabouts used to say they didn't want that tainted money from Washington. Now they're saying, 'Tain't enough.'"

305 Young Tad looked up from the newspaper and asked his farmer daddy, "What are political plums, Pa? Do they grow from seeds?"

"Not always, my boy. Sometimes they're the result of smart grafting."

GRAMMAR

306 Mr. William Monroe, born and raised in an educated family, had graduated the previous June from a very prestigious university. Now he was professor of English at Cedar Ridge High School in the Ozark Mountains. One day he asked a class, "Would you say, 'A hen lays, or a hen lies'?"

Kenny Thompson spoke up. "I'd lift her up to see."

307 A couple from Missouri visited Boston to see the historical sites in the fight for American independence. Late one evening, tired and sleepy, they stopped at a service station. The husband asked the attendant, "Could you tell us a good place to stop at"?

"I would advise," said the attendant, "that while in Boston, you stop just before the 'at'."

GRAVE DIGGERS

308 A grave digger had a terrible quarrel with his wife before going to work. That day he took out his anger on the ground and dug so far down he couldn't climb out. As night began falling he yelled for help. A man heard him call and ran into the graveyard.

"Please, please help me out," the grave digger begged as he looked into the passerby's face. "It's getting cold down here."

To his astonishment, the passerby began shoveling dirt into the hole. "You poor man," the shoveler said. "No wonder you're cold. There's no dirt on you."

GULLIBILITY

309 The famous circus master, P.T. Barnum opened a museum in New York City. Crowds flocked to see the circus exhibits. However, he soon noted that people would pay admission and remain for hours, strolling from room to room, talking and ogling the curios. This prevented newcomers from coming in.

Barnum finally placed a sign over a door, saying TO THE EGRESS. The patrons, expecting a new exhibit, poured through the door and, before they realized what had happened, found themselves back on the street.

HAIR

310 When a man ran out of food for his pet rabbit he called on his neighbor who had just killed a goat. The neighbor generously gave him a few greasy pieces of goat meat. He fed this to the rabbit and the pet died. Then he went charging over to his neighbor's house. "Your greasy kid stuff has plumb ruined my hare," he wailed.

311 Once upon a time grandmothers turned gray. Now they turn into beauty shops and turn blond, or red, or some other color.

HATS

312 First woman: "When I get down in the dumps I go buy a new hat."

Second woman: "Oh, is that where you got the hat you wore to church Sunday?"

313 Wife: (showing her husband a new hat) "Isn't it just too sweet, dear?"

Husband: (frowning) "No. Send it back. It's just too dear, sweet."

HEALTH AND ILLNESS

314 A chronic groaner and complainer moaned to his wife, "Oh, my poor back. How will I make it through this day?"

Wife: "Cheer up. Think of it this way. You're just a day closer to Medicare!"

315 A middle-aged farmer went to a doctor for a long overdue checkup. The doctor's exam included a cardiogram. The farmer was intrigued by the roll of celluloid with the dotted lines going up and down. "May I take this home and let my wife see it?" he asked the doctor. The doctor consented.

His wife was not at home when he returned, so he placed the roll on their old time, antique piano. Suddenly the piano began playing, "Lord, I'm Coming Home."

316 A new immigrant went to the drug store and asked for an over-the-counter medicine which his doctor had suggested he take. "The doc said I didn't need a prescription and I've forgotten the name," he said.

"Can you remember what it sounded like?" asked the pharmacist.

"Like a city in Aingeland," he said.

"London? Southhampton? Coventry? Liverpool?" he was asked.

"That's it," he exclaimed. "Carter's Little Liverpools."

317 A tired, overworked, overweight pig farmer came in for a physical. When it was over, he said, "Doc, how do I stand?"

The doctor shook his head. "I can't figure that out. It's a wonder to me."

318 Five doctors were trying to diagnose the ailment troubling James Smithson, founder of the Smithsonian Institute. When Smithson overheard the five physicians expressing different opinions, he said: "Why don't you perform an autopsy to find out what is the matter with me? I am dying to know what it is."

319 Health and Medicine Glossary:

Vein — conceited.

Artery — study of paintings.

Bacteria — back door of a cafeteria.

Barium — what doctors do when a patient dies.

Caesarean Section — a housing devlepment in Rome.

Cat Scan — kitty search.

Cauterize — Eye contact with a nurse.

Colic — Lassie's cousin.

HEARING

320 After chasing the speeding car for five miles, the state patrolman finally got the errant motorist to pull over to the shoulder of the highway. "Why didn't you stop when I sounded the siren?" the policeman asked.

"Sorry, officer," the man replied, "but I'm a little deaf."

"Well, don't give it a thought," the highway cop said. "You'll get your hearing in court next week."

321 Two oldtimers were seated side by side on a jet plane and arguing politics. One kept missing the whole point of the other's statements. Finally this man shouted, "How can you miss it? It's as simple as A-B-C!"

"Maybe so," the other man said, "but I'm D-E-F."

HEAVEN

322 Little Henry was trying to explain to the neighbor boy that it was wrong to work on Sunday.

"But what about policemen?" the neighbor asked. "They have to work on Sunday. Won't they go to heaven?"

"Certainly not," Joey replied dogmatically. "They won't be needed there."

323 A new arrival entered the pearly gates and was asked by an angel. "How'd you get up here so fast?"

The man coughed. "Flu."

324 A minister was interrupted in an open-air meeting by a heckler who asked, "Parson, do you believe Lot's wife really turned into a pillar of salt?"

"When I get to heaven, I'll ask her," the minister replied.

"What if she isn't there?" retorted the

heckler.
"Then you ask her."

---

325   A small boy was in New York City for the first time and was being whisked up the elevator in the Empire State Building. As they sped past the 50th floor, he asked his father, "Daddy, does God know we're coming?"

HILLBILLIES

326   Two 19th century West Virginia hillbillies, who had never seen the ocean before, made a trip by horseback to the Atlantic coast. They saw a lighthouse under construction and decided to camp and see what happened next. A few days later it was completed.

That night a dense fog rolled in and the lighthouse siren blew continuously. The two hillbillies sat quietly by their campfire for a long while, then one muttered, "The light shines."

"Yeah and the bell rings," said the other.

"And the horn blows."

"Yep, and the ole fog rolls in jist the same."

HONEYMOONERS

327   A shy bride whispered to her new husband as they entered a hotel lobby. "Let's act as if we've been married five years."

"Okay," he agreed. "But can you manage all three of our suitcases?"

328 Just at dusk the touring honeymooners parked their car and new trailer in a small wooded area by the roadside. The wife looked shyly at her husband and said softly, "Dear, do you remember that flat rock we used for a doorstep at last night's stop? Well, I left the key to the trailer under it."

HONORS

329 Abraham Lincoln was asked how he liked being President of the United States. He replied with the story of a man who was tarred and feathered and rode out of town on a rail. Someone asked the man how he liked such treatment and he replied, "If it wasn't for the honor of the thing, I'd much rather walk."

HORSES

330 An Easterner stopped off at a Western ranch and watched some cowboys doing some fancy riding and roping. "I'm not impressed," he said laughing.

A cowboy flipped him the reins of a pony and said, "You show us, pardner."

The Easterner had taken some riding lessons and swung aboard. A moment later he was picking himself up out of the dust.

"What happened?" the cowboy asked pleasantly. "What threw you, pardner?"

"What threw me? Didn't you see this wild horse buck?" cried the Easterner.

"Buck? Whaddya mean? That pony only

coughed."

---

331 Lincoln often told about a Kentucky boy who kept trotting a horse back and forth for a prospective buyer to look over.

Finally, the man complained, "This horse has got splints."

"Mister," the boy replied, scratching his head., "I don't know what splints is, but if it's good for him he's got 'em, and if it ain't good for him he ain't got 'em."

HOSPITALS

332 Glossary and Definition of Hospital Terms

Enema — opposite of a friend.

Fester — quick treatment.

Hangnail — pot hook.

Medical staff — physician's cane.

Nitrates — less than day rates.

Pelvis — cousin to Elvis.

Recovery room — where they do upholstery.

Seizure — What Mrs. Caesar said to her husband when their daughter was running away.

Tumor — more than one.

Urine — opposite of you're out.

HOTELS

333 Aunt Hettie was spending her first night in a hotel. "This way, ma'am," directed the porter as the door opened before them.

"But there's no bed in this tiny room," Aunt

Hettie complained. "I can't sleep here."

"Ma'am," said the porter. "This is only the elevator."

---

334 A small hotel in a county seat town advertised that there wasn't a single cockroach anywhere on the premises. But one of the guests moved out the same day he had registered. Later he sent the hotel owner a letter charging false advertising.

"I told the truth," the hotel man said. "There isn't a single cockroach in my place. They're all married and have big families."

---

335 A businessman was caught overnight in a seedy looking town. He went to the one hotel and took his pen to register. As he signed his name a huge bedbug crawled across the desk.

"Wow!" he whistled to the clerk. "I've been in lots of hotels, and I've been bitten by some smart bedbugs, but never have I found one that came to find out the number of my room."

---

336 Country boy Charlie was showing off his learning to his teacher: "Did you know that Mr. Hilton is going to buy the Leaning Tower of Pisa and turn it into a hotel?"

"No," the teacher said taking him seriously.

"Yeah. He's gonna call it, 'The Tilton Hilton.'"

HOUSES

337 Two tycoons were talking about their climb from rags to riches. Said one, "Our house was so little that when papa dropped his toupee, we had wall-to-wall carpeting."

HUNTERS AND HUNTING

338 A rich but inexperienced hunter wanted to make a trip to Africa and called on an experienced hunter for advice. "Hunt for tigers only at night," he was urged. "Then you can see their eyes blazing and all you need do is put a bullet between their eyes."

When the neophyte hunter, bruised and barely alive, returned six weeks later, the old hunter asked how he did and got a negative response. "Didn't you hunt for tigers at night?" the old hunter asked. "Didn't you look for their shining eyes and didn't you shoot them between the eyes?"

"I did all that," the new hunter said, "but the tigers are smarter than when you were there. They now walk in pairs and each keeps one eyes closed."

339 It was deer-hunting season and several hunters from the big city were sitting around a pot-bellied stove in an Ozark store sharing experiences. Finally, a local man said, "I'm not impressed with stories about you city fellers hittin' deer from three and four hundred yards off. Why, last Friday, I was a-walkin' along the trail when these sharp eyes of mine spotted a twelve-point buck. I rammed a charge down my gun barrel, then put in some wadding and a few ounces of salt. Then I pulled the trigger. Bang! That old buck dropped in his tracks."

"Very interesting, old timer," said one of the sportsmen from Little Rock. "But why did you put salt in your gun?"

"Shucks, Bud, that buck was so fur off, I had to do somethin' to keep the meat from spoilin' before I could git there."

---

340 An Arkansas guide took his new minister on a duck-hunting trip and returned exhausted from a long day in the blinds. While he was resting one of the church deacons dropped by.

"Is our new reverend a good shot?" the deacon asked.

Not wishing to be critical, the duck hunter replied, "A fine shot, but it's a wonder how the Lord protects the birds from him."

---

341 Sign in a store window in a southern Missouri hamlet: "Closed Because of Illness. Buck Fever." It was deer season.

---

342 A city sportsman roared into a small North Arkansas town with his van loaded with hunting gear. "Is there good hunting around here?" he asked a man in overalls sitting on a store porch.

"Shore," said the mountain man, "there's plenty of huntin' but not much findin'."

343 A Baptist deacon was determined to go hunting on the last day of the deer season even if it was Sunday. His wife pleaded with him in vain. He went on and while walking through a rocky hollow got stuck in a narrow crevice between two boulders. He struggled to get free, but his efforts seemed only to wedge his body more tightly in the crevice. He had terrible thoughts of never getting free.

Along about eleven o'clock, his wife's face began swimming before his eyes. He thought of all he had failed to do. He thought of his wife and children sitting in church. Within ten minutes he felt so small that he was able to wiggle through to freedom.

344 Two city dudes arrived in the Arkansas Ozarks for a bear hunt. Soon they came across the footprints of a huge brown bear. "You go on and see where he went," said one.

"What are you going to do while I'm gone?" asked the other.

"I'll backtrack to see where he came from."

345 Bill Huddelston, the rich lumber mill owner in a Missouri town, returned from a safari to Africa and began telling about bagging a lion.

"You really bagged a lion?" his impressed postmaster neighbor asked.

"Sure did. There I was separated from my

guide in the tall grass. Suddenly the king of the beasts appeared within ten feet of me. I bagged and bagged until he went away."

---

346 Said Ozark Ike, the famous bear hunter: "As that 600-pound bear charged at me, I was standing under a big white oak. I leaped for a branch 20 feet above the ground."

"Did you make it, Ike?" chorused the boys in the country store.

"Not on the way up, but to my good health I managed to grab it on the way down."

---

347 A party of hunters who went out looking for a wild boar for meat. When the boar suddenly sprang upon them, all of the men except one climbed trees to get away. The one who remained on the ground seized the ferocious, snorting animal and undertook to hold him. After holding the boar for several minutes, the man felt his strength giving way. "Boys," he yelled to the men in the trees, "ya've gotta come down and help me let go!"

HUSBANDS

348 Several women were voicing opinions about their husbands. One said, "My husband is a very thoughtful man. He thinks twice before saying nothing."

---

349 Two young women were discussing what

they wanted in a husband. Said one, "I want to marry a go-getter."

"Not me," retorted the other. "I want an already-gotter."

350 Sunday school teacher to her class of young women: "How many of you girls would like to have husbands?" All raised their hands.

"That's bad," she said. "I suggest you leave the husbands alone and go after the single men."

351 A husband and wife were taking a second honeymoon. When they reached the airport the husband sighed, "I wish I had brought along my fishing tackle box."

"Why do you wish that?" his wife asked. "You promised me that you wouldn't talk about fishing for a whole week."

"I know. It's just that I bought the tickets when I went through town to get to the lake last week. And I forgot to take them out of my tackle box when we left home this morning."

352 On his way home from work, Smitty stopped and had coffee with a work buddy. After awhile, he said, "I've gotta mosey along home and explain to Sarah."

"Explain what?" his buddy asked.

"Can't tell you now," replied Smitty, getting into his coat. "I won't know til I get home and she starts quizzing me."

353 Sign at Crossroads Church Rummage Sale: "Your chance to rid your house of everything not worth keeping, but too valuable to throw away. Bring your husband."

354 A group of married women whose husbands had well-paying jobs were having lunch one day. They went around the table naming their favorite authors. One named her husband.

"Oh," the others gushed. "We didn't know your husband was a writer. What does he write?"

"Checks."

355 A mother thought her children had been acting too rebellious. "I'm going to give two dollars to the most obedient member of the family next week," she promised.

"Aw, Mama," protested six-year-old Gloria. "Pa will win that easy."

356 A factory worker asked his foreman if he could have the day off to help his wife with her spring house-cleaning.

"Certainly not," the foreman said. "I can't let you stay home for an excuse like that."

"That's great," said the worker. "Thanks a lot. I knew I could count on you in a pinch."

357 A husband was telling his cronies, "Me, I make all the big decisions in my family and leave my wife with the little ones. She decides what kind of car to buy, how much I spend on clothes, when and where I go fishing. I decide important matters like who the Republicans and Democrats will nominate for president next year."

358 Errands are what a boy runs before 15 and what a man runs after he's married.

359 A lion tamer in the circus feared nothing on earth except his wife. One evening he was out so late he was afraid to go home. The next morning his wife discovered he was missing and became worried. She called the police, his friends, and finally set out to search the town. She found him at the circus sleeping in a lion's cage, his head pillowed against a huge lion's neck.

He awoke to see her looking at him through the bars of the cage. "You coward!" she snarled. "You didn't dare face me."

360 A woman called the missing persons bureau and reported the absence of her husband. "If we find him," the policewoman said, "what shall we tell him?"

The woman said, "Tell him mother decided

not to come until next year."

HYMNS

361 Years ago the sole employee, an engineer, on duty at a country radio station on Sunday morning, had the job of selecting a suitable recording to introduce a preacher's sermon. On this occasion, he chose a number titled, "You'd Better Get Down on Your Knees."

The preacher positioned himself before the microphone and announced the hymn. The engineer spun the record and the audience heard:

"You'd better get down on your knees
An' roll them bones, boys,
'Cause baby needs a new pair of shoes!"

HYPOCRITES

362 A preacher visited a farmer to invite him to church. "I wouldn't go to your church if it was the last church on earth," said the farmer. "I know a fellow down there and he isn't as good as me. He's a hypocrite."

Several months passed. The preacher called on the farmer again. "I want to buy a hog," he said.

The farmer showed him his best hogs. Then the preacher spotted a runt rooting in the dirt near the side of the barn. "I want to buy that one," he said.

The farmer couldn't understand why and tried to argue with the preacher. Finally he agreed to sell the runt and put him in the preacher's truck. "What are you going to do with that runt?" the farmer asked, as the preacher started to pull away."

The preacher yelled out the truck window. "I'm going to drive all over this area and tell people this is the kind of hogs you raise."

The farmer became angry. "That's not fair. Most of my hogs are big, fine-looking animals. That little runt isn't."

The preacher called back, "What's fair for the church is fair for the hogs."

IGNORANCE

363 The great scientist, Albert Einstein, was traveling by train to Princeton University. In the dining car he realized he had forgotten his glasses and could not read the menu without them. He called the waiter and asked him to read the menu.

The waiter took the menu card and turned it this way and that. Finally he turned to the discoverer of the theory of relativity and said, "Ah, can't make it out, suh. Ah'm afraid Ah'm jist as ignorant as you am."

INDIANS

364 Two Amazon Indians crept out of the jungle to the river's edge and spotted their first waterskier.

"Why man make big canoe go so fast?" one asked.

"Big chief on vine chase 'em."

365 Long ago an Indian chief of the west, in a state that would one day be called Colorado, was about to die. He called for Geronimo and Fallen Rocks, the two bravest warriors in the tribe, and asked them to go out and seek deer skins. The one returning with the most skins would be the new chief. Geronimo came back several weeks later with 200 skins. Fallen Rocks never returned. To this day as you drive through Colorado, you see signs saying, "Watch out for fallen rocks."

366 An Indian chief appeared before a judge in Arizona asking that his name be shortened. "What is your name now?" the judge asked.
"Chief Screeching Train Whistle."
"How do you wish it shortened?"
"To Toots, Your Honor."

367 A tourist stopped to buy some Ozark crafts and asked the storekeeper if he thought it would rain.
"We're gonna have a big 'un," the country merchant said.
The prediction turned out to be accurate. On his next trip into the hills, the tourist sought the storekeeper out again. "Dunno about the weather this time," he said. "TV's broke."

368 One Indian to another: "Where's that

pioneer you just shot?"

"Over there," he replied, "just follow the arrow."

---

369 A distinguished Sioux Indian chief came to Washington and visited the vice president. He looked the veep straight in the eye and said, "I hope you'll be careful with your immigration laws. We were too careless with ours."

---

370 Many years ago the Lone Ranger and his "faithful Indian companion," Tonto were riding through the hills of Wyoming. Suddenly, the Lone Ranger spotted a band of wild Apache Indians coming toward them from the south. "Turn north," he hollered to Tonto.

"No, go west," the Lone Ranger corrected, "Wild Sioux comin' from the north."

Seconds later, they saw wild Indians from another tribe bearing down on them from the west. "Go east," the Long Ranger ordered.

They whirled their horses around only to face another band sweeping in from the east. The Lone Ranger pulled back on Silver's reins. As the horse reared in the air, the Lone Ranger asked, "What are we gonna do, Tonto?"

Tonto replied, "Whatta ya mean 'we', white man?"

---

371 Moe: "Why did Oklahoma first belong to the Indians?"

Joe: "They got their reservation in first."

IINGENUITY

372 You're trapped in a steel cell with only a mirror and a table. How could you get out?

First, look in the looking glass and see what you saw. Second, take the saw and cut the table in half. Third, put the two halves together and make a whole. Fourth, crawl out the whole.

INSECTS

373 Two big mosquitoes were nibbling on Robinson Crusoe's back. One finally said, "I've had enough for today. Let's get together on Friday."

INSURANCE

374 A farmer's barn burned down and the insurance claims agent explained that the company would build him another barn instead of paying the claim in cash. The farmer was furious. "If that's the way you insurance people do business, then cancel the policy I've got on my wife."

375 A cantankerous husband took out insurance on every member of his family except himself. When queried about this, he told the insurance agent, "When I pass on, I want everybody to be miserable."

376 An insurance salesman was talking to a prospective customer. "Madam," he said, "if you

should lose your husband, what would you get?"
"A parakeet," she replied.

INTRODUCTIONS

377 Said the lightning bug when he flew into the ceiling fan: "I'm de-lighted to be here."

378 Cousin Pete says: "Some people won't put their right foot forward until they get the left one in hot water."

379 A politician started his speech by saying, "My address may be like an old-time hoopskirt. It would cover the object but not touch the subject. Or would you prefer it be like the modern fashion? It would touch the object but not cover the subject."

380 The announcer was introducing the radio preacher. "The man you are about to hear present the Word of God has been a household sound, going out across the airways to uncounted millions of hearers. We can use one of the great phrases of Scripture in introducing Reverend Buck Jones. He's 'the prince of the powers of the air.' "

381 When Will Rogers went to the White House he was taken to the Oval Office to meet the elected leader of America. "Mr. Rogers," the aide said, "this is our distinguished president, Mr. Calvin Coolidge."

"Pardon me," Rogers said, "but I didn't get the name."

***

382 Introductions are like perfume. They are to be inhaled, but never swallowed.

INVENTORS

383 A clever chemist made a soft drink formula and tried marketing it under the name of "One-up." When it didn't sell, he changed the name to "Two-up," then "Three-up," and on up to "Six-up," when he became discouraged and gave up.

He never knew how close he came to success.

INVESTORS

384 A discouraged farmer-investor faced his county seat broker. "You just have to be patient, Harvey," the broker said. "Your stocks will go up some day."

"At the rate the stocks you sold me are going," Harvey said, "I'll be a patient before they do go up."

IRISHMEN

385 A native of upstate New York was showing an Irish visitor the wonder of Niagara Falls. He rattled off the statistics, how far the water falls, the total gallons of water that go over the falls each second, and on and on until the Irishman was plainly bored. At last the New Yorker turned to the visitor from Ireland and said, "There isn't a wonder like this in the whole world, don't you think?"

The unimpressed Irishman grunted and said, "Aye. Maybe so. But what's to stop it?"

JOBS

386 A country boy came to the manager of a new service station built beside the new highway and asked for a job.

"Sorry, no openings," said the man.

"Mister," the job seeker persisted, "don't you ever think about the hereafter?"

"What's that got to do with a job for you?" replied the manager.

"Everything. A job is what I'm here after!"

387 The personnel director of the new plant in a rural town was interviewing Clark for a job. One of the questions he asked was, "Are you a clockwatcher?"

"No, sir," Cousin Clark replied. "I've never had an inside job. I'm a whistle listener."

KISSING

388 During World War II a colonel, a private, an elderly woman and a beautiful young blonde girl found themselves seated together on a train. The colonel and the private sat facing the two ladies.

While going through a long, dark tunnel the overhead lights blinked out. Suddenly there came the sound of a kiss and a slap. When the lights came on, the colonel's face was still stinging. "That insolent private," he said to himself. "He kissed the girl and she slapped me."

The elderly lady could hardly disguise a grin as she thought to herself, "That silly private tried to kiss the girl and she slapped him."

The girl was trying hard not to giggle as she thought, "That private doesn't have a very good sense of direction. Instead of kissing me, he kissed the old woman and she slapped him."

The private had to grit his teeth to keep from laughing out loud about what he would tell his pals when he got back to the base: "I kissed the back of my hand and slapped the colonel."

LANDLORDS

389 "Why don't you ask your landlord to fix that loose board on your porch?" a visitor asked.

"No way," the tenant replied. "He'd figure out some way to charge us extra. The last time we told him the roof leaked, he charged us two bucks a day for shower baths."

LATENESS

390 The boss frowned as the perpetually late worker walked in. "What's the excuse this time, Jenkins?" he growled.

"Well, it's this way, boss. Nine people slept at our house last night and the alarm was only set for eight."

LAWMEN

391 This was the third time the state patrolman had stopped Jake for speeding. "What am I gonna do with this ticket?" Jake grumbled.

"When the judge gets through with you, frame it. When you get five, you get a mule."

392 The officer stopped a woman who was late bringing her son to school. "Soon as I saw you coming," the cop said, "I figured you were approaching 55 in this school zone."

The woman glared back. "How dare you speak that way of a young woman."

393 Deputy Barney Bradley's patience was running thin with the movie people who acted like they owned the little town of Jaybird. He had warned them a dozen times to slow down. When he clocked the star actress going 20 miles too fast, he pulled her over with a flourish and started writing.

Before he could complete a line, she grabbed his book, smiled sweetly, signed her autograph and sped away.

394 When the officer finished writing the ticket for driving under the influence, he said, "That will keep you off the road for six months."

The drunk replied, "But, officer, my living depends on it."

"Yes, but so does everyone else's!"

395 A young police cadet was asked, "If you were alone in a police car and being pursued by a gang of bank robbers at 70 miles an hour, what would you do?"

"Eighty," he replied.

396 The FBI sent out six different pictures of a "most wanted" escaped convict. Three days later they got back this telegram from a small town deputy: "HOLDING FIVE IN JAIL. ON TRAIL OF THE SIXTH."

397 A dog and a cat began scrapping in a roadside honkytonk. A drunk suddenly pulled his gun and shot the cat. The sheriff heard the shot and came racing in.

"Shhhh," whispered the drunk to the customers as the sheriff was arriving. "Don't squeal on me. He'll think the dog did it."

398 The policeman pulled the bleeding man to his feet. "Now, sir, describe the man who hit you, and I'll find him."

Man: "Officer, that's what I was doing when he hit me."

399 The town never seemed to have enough money to replace the one old Chevrolet which the part-time deputy drove. The deputy decided to do something about it. He stopped the mayor and began writing out a ticket for speeding.

"But I was within the limit," the motorist pleaded.

"Sure, Your Honor," the deputy admitted, "but I can't catch up with the drivers who go over the limit."

400 A motorcycle cop stopped a woman for speeding on a busy freeway. As he scribbled out the ticket, the woman growled, "Why don't you police officers spend your time catching reckless, crazy drivers that cause accidents?"

The officer nodded. "Just have," he said, as he handed her the ticket.

401 "But, officer," the speeding motorist pleaded. "I didn't hear your siren."

"Of course. Of course, of course," muttered the policeman. "You were past the sound barrier."

LAWYERS

402 The long-winded lawyer droned until the judge gave a meaningful yawn. "I trust, Your Honor," said the lawyer, "that I'm not engaging in a trespass on the important time of this noble court."

"There is a difference," the judge solemnly noted, "between trespassing on time and encroaching on eternity."

403 The defense and prosecution lawyers became embroiled in a name calling contest. The defense yelled, "You are a lowdown crook and so phony you couldn't get a job in a parrot's show."

"And you are a cheap shyster who can be bought by the worst criminals in the world," screamed the prosecution."

The judge banged his gavel. "That's enough. Now that the learned counsel have identified themselves, let us continue the case."

404 A poor lawyer said to a busy, successful one: "Brother, can you spare a crime?"

405 A young lawyer asked a veteran judge for advice. Said the judge: "If you're strong on the law and weak on the facts, elaborate on the law."

"What if I'm weak on both law and facts?" said the young lawyer.

"Then bang on the table."

406 One lawyer was speaking to another about a third attorney. "Johnson has chased ambulances so much that he speaks to the jury with a slight accident."

407 A lawyer's wife was complaining that they needed new furniture. "Be patient, honey," he assured her. "A man is coming to talk to me about a divorce tomorrow. He's pretty well fixed. As soon as I can break up his home, I'll fix up ours."

408 A lawyer was asked what his fee was to handle a burglary case. "One thousand dollars and twelve steak dinners," he said.

"What's the steak dinners for?" the accused man asked.

"Listen, when I defend you, I'll have the jury eating out of my hands."

409 On a lawyer's tombstone this epitaph was carved: "Here lies a lawyer and an honest man."

A few days later someone came and chalked underneath the epitaph: "Two people buried in one coffin."

LIARS

410 A man got on a bus and stooped down to pick up a coin while the other passengers watched him. Cupping the big coin in his hand, he said, "Did anyone here lose a half dollar?"

Several responded, "I did."

"Well," the finder said, "Here's a nickel of it." And he handed a five cent piece to the nearest man.

LOYALTY

411 Many young soldiers, for various reasons, slipped away from the Union Army during the terrible Civil War. Lincoln tended to treat absent-without-leave cases with much leniency. "If the good Lord has given a man a cowardly pair of legs," he said, "it is difficult to keep them from running away with him."

MAGICIANS AND MEDIUMS

412 Two retired magicians were talking over old times. "Say, whatever happened to that pretty assistant of yours?" asked one. "You know, the one you used to cut in half?"

"She's been doing fine. Since our last show, she's been living in Nashville and Little Rock.

---

413 A magician was hired to entertain passengers on a Mississippi River cruise ship. A passenger brought a parrot aboard which immediately began to question the magician's skills. Each time the magician started to do a trick, the parrot would squawk, "Phoney! Phoney!"

This went on for several days, with the parrot continuing to yell, "Phoney! Phoney! while the cruise ship and its passengers moved down the river from St. Louis to New Orleans. Unfortunately, when the ship reached New Orleans, a horrendous hurricane blew in from the Gulf. The ship capsized in the middle of the night and sank, leaving the passengers to scramble for lifeboats, planks, and anything else that would float.

The parrot found himself clinging to one end of a plank. In the darkness that was illumined only by a pale quarter moon, the parrot could make out the magician clinging to the other end of the plank.

The plank floated downriver toward the ocean gulf. When day came, the magician saw the parrot staring speechless at him. Another day and night passed. Finally on the third morning, the parrot squawked loudly: "All right, wise guy, whatja do with the ship?"

414 A seven-year-old boy kept disturbing a medium during a seance. Finally the medium asked impatiently, "What do you want, sonny?"

"I wanna speak with Grandma," he begged.

"All right," said the medium and began her mumbo-jumbo routine, "Grandma's comin'," the faker assured. "Your grandma's comin'. There she is!"

"Grandma," squealed the boy. "What are you doin' here? You aren't dead yet."

MAIDS

415 Nellie Bradbury was the new maid hired by Squire Hanson's wife, Elizabeth, in Montgomery, Alabama. When Nellie was told to prepare a meal for visitors, she asked her mistress, "How would you like it served, Miss Elizabeth?"

"What do you mean by that?" her employer asked.

"I mean, do you want me to serve them so they'll come again or so they'll stay away?"

MANNERS

416 Madeline Hampton, a wealthy society lady in Mississippi, had difficulty with her upper denture. When she talked it often slipped down without her being aware of it. For a special dinner, she asked her butler to watch her mouth and when the denture began slipping to say, "The maid is at the door."

During the dinner, "Miss" Madeline began talking and the plate began slipping. "The maid is at the door," the butler said three times.

Finally she looked up. "Did you call me, Jenkins?"

"Yes, Madam, I said 'The maid is at the door.' But she's in the punch bowl now."

⸻

417 Waiter: "May I help you out of that soup, sir?"

Uncouth customer: "I'm not in the soup! What did you mean by that remark?"

Waiter: "But, sir, from the sound, I thought you might need to be dragged ashore."

⸻

418 Uncle George decided to take advantage of a sale at the Penney store and buy Aunt Geraldine three pairs of nylons. After waiting an hour on the fringe of a screaming, pushing mob of females, he plunged toward the counter with both arms flailing. Suddenly a shrill voice hollered, "Can't you act like a gentleman?"

"I've been acting like a gentleman for over an hour, and it got me nowhere," Uncle George snorted, as he kept plowing toward the counter.

"Now I'm going to act like a lady!"

419 Abner, a boy from the backwoods, read up on etiquette when he got to college. When he felt fully capable of good manners he invited a girl to have dinner with him in a fashionable restaurant. He ate slowly and was very careful to practice good manners.

After the dessert, Abner reached for a toothpick, used it a moment, then put it back in the container . He smiled at yhe girl and said, "I'll bet some people steal them little sticks."

420 Ben: "I'm invited to a banquet. Should I eat chicken with my fingers."

Min: "No, eat your fingers separately."

MARRIAGE

421 "Our honeymoon is over," remarked the young bridegroom.

"How can you tell?" his friend asked.

"There are more bills than coos."

422 "Are you a man or a mouse?" a husband was asked.

"I am both a mouse and the head of my house," he replied.

"But how can you be a mouse and the head of your house?"

"My wife is scared of mice."

423 Marriage counselor to husband: "Don't you and your wife ever have a difference of opinion?"

"Certainly, but I don't tell her."

424 A wealthy old widower took as his second wife a girl 50 years younger than himself. Asked why he risked the difference, the octogenarian replied, "I'd rather spend the rest of my life smelling perfume than liniment."

425 An elderly couple of pioneer days frequently argued. When their spats were finished, no matter who won, the wife would move to the south end of the porch and pout. The husband would do the same at the north end. Sometimes they would go for days without speaking.

One hot summer day, after an especially heated wrangle, a wagon pulled by two yoked oxen passed before their house. The wife remarked plaintively, "Pa, look at them oxen. "Why can't we walk side by side and pull together on the road of life like them?"

The disgruntled husband grumbled his answer, "Maybe we could, Ma, if we only had one tongue between us."

426 Joe arrived home a day late from a business trip and suddenly recalled that he had forgotten to call his wife and tell her not to come and get him at the airport the day before. He was too scared to call home from the airport, so he took a taxi. He had the driver drop him off two blocks away. As he sneaked in through the backyard, he spotted his wife pacing up and down. "Don't pay the ransom, honey!" he shouted. "I escaped!"

427 Two husbands were comparing notes on their wives. Said one, "My wife sometimes dreams she's married to a millionaire."

"You're lucky," replied the other. "That's what my wife thinks when she's awake."

428 A girl shouldn't marry the man in the moon for four good reasons: (1) He has "cheesy" tastes. (2) He makes only a quarter a week. (3) He gets "full" every month. (4) Every night he stays out later than the night before.

429 Two women friends were chatting after a long separation. "Tell me," said one, "has your husband lived up to the promise he made when courting you."

"He certainly has. He told me then he wasn't good enough for me, and he's been proving it ever since."

430 Jack: "My wife believes she needs a dishwasher."

Zack: "Good for you. My wife believes she married one."

---

431 Two women were gossiping in the beauty parlor. "The talk is that Jane married that Henry Simpson because his uncle left him a million," said one.

"Now really," said the other, "I don't think Jane is that kind of girl. She'd have married him no matter who left the money to him."

---

432 Young husband to bride: "Sweet, my mama could teach you a few things about how to make homemade bread."

Bride: "I'm sure she could, and while we're on the subject of parents, my daddy could teach you a few things about how to make dough."

---

433 "Marriage is like a railroad sign," said recently wed Jed. "You see a pretty girl coming. You stop and look. And after you're married, you listen."

---

434 A fellow came to his doctor for an examination. "I'm getting married," he said, "and would like to have my head examined."

---

435 A new bride was applying for a job and came to the place where the application asked, "How long do you expect to work?"

She answered, "From here to maternity."

436 A young husband stopped his minister at the door of the church. "Would it be right," he asked, "for one person to profit from the mistake of another?"

The minister shook his head.

"Then, sir, would it be possible for you to return the $20 I gave you when you married me last June?"

437 Two married women met at a class reunion. "What type of husband did you get?" asked one.

"Well, I'll tell you this. If he talks about roses and daisies in his sleep, he's definitely talking about flowers."

438 A man and wife sat down in the marriage counselor's office. "What's her name here says I'm forgetful," complained the man.

439 Warning to wives: Don't henpeck your husband or you might find him listening to other chicks.

440 A young woman and her fiancee were applying for a marriage license. "Seems silly to be getting a license now," she mumbled. "The hunting season is over for me."

441 A henpecked electrician had received an emergency call from the Smith's residence. When he rang the bell, both Smith and his wife met him at the door. Being a very methodical man, Smith said, "Before you go up in the attic and look at the wiring, I wish to acquaint you with my difficulties."

The electrician held out his hand meekly to Mrs. Smith and said, "Happy to meet you, ma'am."

442 A young married couple were having their first quarrel when the wife burst into tears. "You promised if I married you," she wailed, "you'd be humbly grateful."

"Well, so what," he growled back.

"Well, you're not," she replied. "You've turned out to be grumbly hateful."

443 A man and his brother and their wives were out for a ride. The man's wife and sister-in-law sat in the back seat giving him driving instructions. Finally, he snorted, "From now on sit up here. I don't like women to drive from the back seat."

"Humph!" his wife snorted back. "We're no worse than men who cook from the kitchen table."

444 "Do you believe you can support my

daughter in the manner to which she is accustomed in this household?" the father asked the suitor.

"No, sir," he answered frankly, "but I'll soon accustom her to the manner in which I can support her."

445 A thrifty young woman became concerned about the amount of money her boy friend was spending on her. After one expensive date, she asked her mother, "What can I do to stop Jerry from spending so much money on me."

Her mother replied simply, "Marry him."

446 Company was coming and Willy's wife persuaded him to help with house cleaning on his day off from the plant. The phone rang and Willy switched off the vacuum cleaner to answer, "Hello, this is Labor. Management is taking a soap opera break."

447 A family was a half day away from home on their summer vacation when six-year-old Jenny asked from the back seat, "Daddy, before you married Mommy, who told you how to drive?"

448 A wife was complaining to her husband about the changes in her life since they had married. "I enjoyed the life of a social butterfly before I married you," she recalled.

"Yes," said her husband, "and it looks like you've changed into a moth the way you go through new clothes."

449 "Darling," said the young wife, "when you proposed, you said I should never want for a thing."

"Ah, yes," said the husband. "But I was ignorant then of how much you could want."

450 Old Prophet Pete says whether a man winds up with a nest egg or a goose egg will depend on the chick he marries.

451 Red Skeleton was talking about marriage when he said, "If a girl has never been married, she should wear a white gown. If she has been married once before, she should wear a blue gown. If it's her third trip up the aisle, she should wear a white dress trimmed in blue. As for Liz Taylor, she's gonna look silly comin' down that aisle in a crazy quilt."

452 A young bachelor came into a jewelry store. "I'd like to see a ring," he said.

The salesman showed him several engagement rings, then suggested, "You can save money on a combination set."

"What do you mean?" asked the bachelor.

"Three for the price of two. Engagement, wedding and teething."

453 Two opposing politicians were in the midst of a hot debate. Charges and countercharges flew thick and fast. Finally one yelled at the other, "How do you explain the powerful interests that call every move you make?"

The other man fired back, "You keep my wife out of this."

MEN

454 "Hey, didja hear there was a man-eatin' shark sighted in the bay yesterday?" the resort visitor asked her girl friend.

"Yeah, but who's worried? He'll die of starvation around here."

MERCHANTS

455 Sign in a Chicago tailor shop: "Hurry Right in, Folks. There's a Man in Here Having a Fit Right This Minute."

456 In a southern town three competing businessmen had their clothing stores side by side. In the spirit of competition, each held a fall sale on the same days. This fall they had advertised in the newspapers, prepared posters and displayed goods in their store windows. At five a.m. on the morning the sale was due to begin, the merchant in the middle erected this sign over his doorway: MAIN ENTRANCE

~~~~~~~~~~~~~~~~~~~~~~~~~~~~~~~~~~~~~~

457 The department store manager's phone rang at one a.m. He sleepily answered the fifth ring. "This is Mrs. Elizabeth Hathaway. I'm one of your customers and am just calling to tell you how lovely that suit is I bought at your store last week."

"That's fine," the manager mumbled, fighting to keep his temper under control, "but why did you call me up at this hour to tell me?"

"Because," the customer said sweetly, "your truck just dropped it off."

~~~~~~~~~~~~~~~~~~~~~~~~~~~~~~~~~~~~~~

458 Bill brought home his semester report card in January and his merchant father asked for an explanation of the low grades. "Dad, the boy said, "I'm following your example. You always mark things down after the holidays."

~~~~~~~~~~~~~~~~~~~~~~~~~~~~~~~~~~~~~~

459 A tourist from the big city stopped at a roadside grocery in Hope, Arkansas and picked up a watermelon. "And what's the price of this little cantaloupe?" he asked the clerk.

Without blinking, the clerk said, "Pardon me, Sir, but you must have poor eyesight. That's only an olive."

~~~~~~~~~~~~~~~~~~~~~~~~~~~~~~~~~~~~~~

460 A man walked into a clothing store in Birmingham and called, "Hey, Jerry, I was sorry to hear about your big fire."

"Keep your voice down," replied the

manager. "It's not until Thursday."

<hr>

461 A tourist ran into a crossroads general store and found the owner, a bewhiskered old fellow, slouched in an old rocker by a pot-bellied stove.

"I need some fish hooks in a hurry," said the tourist. "The fish are really biting down at the lake."

"So what?" grumbled the oldster. "Don't get so excited, young feller."

"Hurry up and wait on me," the tourist demanded.

"That will take a little doin'," said the old man as he kept rocking. "You should have come in when I was standin' up."

MILITARY SERVICE

462 Little boy, bragging about his dad's new stripe: "The longer he stays in the army, the ranker he gets."

Boy's mother: "I agree."

<hr>

463 Joe Dope arrived in Marine Camp and found a mile-long line waiting to be fed. A sergeant spotted him and yelled, "Go to the end of the line."

Thirty minutes later, Joe returned. "How can I, Sarge? There's somebody already there."

<hr>

464 An Army cook had just cooked up a huge

order of boiled eggs for a mob of recruits. While the soldiers gobbled up the eggs, he sat down and wrote to his gal: "Dearest, for two hours shells have been bursting all around me."

465 The entire neighborhood was wondering how a local boy, who had been spoiled with special privileges by his parents, was making out in the Army. When the boy's mother received a letter, her neighbors converged on the house. They knew the boy had been given every luxury at home and wondered how he was faring. "How's Brian making out?" they asked eagerly.

"Just fine," the doting mother reported. "He says they're making him a court marshall and the general is presiding at the ceremonies."

466 Sergeant Barker stepped into the barracks and called out to the recruits, "Any of you guys know shorthand?"

Two privates stepped forward, anticipating being transferred to lighter duties.

"Well," the sergeant said, "go help the mess sergeant with the potato peeling. He's short-handed today."

467 A worm joined the Army. They put him in the apple corps.

468 Two corporals stopped after they ran over

an animal with their jeep. "We smashed it pretty bad," one said. "But I can tell it has stripes."

"Yeah," said the other. "It must be either a skunk or a drill sergeant."

~~~~~~

469 The elite new nuclear aircraft carrier was in port and the crew were receiving visitors at an "open house." A young sailor had the job of showing an inquisitive woman around and trying to answer her numerous questions about the operation of the carrier.

"Now, young man," she said, "what in the world would you do if the ship should spring a leak?"

"That wouldn't be a big problem, ma'am," said the bored sailor. "We'd just put a bucket under it."

~~~~~~

470 "Attention, squad," the drill sergeant yelled to his awkward recruits. "Lift your right leg and hold it straight out before you."

One private mistakenly held up his left leg, bringing it out side by side with his neighbor's right leg.

"All right," shouted the sergeant, "who is that nitwit back there holding up both legs?"

~~~~~~

471 An Army captain was promoted to major and given a new office. The first day a private knocked on the door and asked to speak to him. Wanting to impress the private of his promotion and impressive office, the major picked up his phone and began talking..."Yes, see you at the time suggested. Thank you, General..."

The private interrupted. "Sir," he blurted.

"Can't you tell I was on the phone with the general?"

"Yes, but...."

"Now what can I do for you?" the major asked impatiently.

"If you please, sir, I've come to connect your phone with the outside line."

472 The smart young thing asked the soldier she met at a party during the Vietnam War. "What's your rank?"

"PFC," he replied.

"What's that?"

"Praying for civilian."

473 A Marine private got acquainted with a girl in the PX. "See that ugly, long-nosed officer, over there," he said. "He's in charge of our battalion, and the meanest officer we ever had."

"Yes, I see him," said the girl. "He happens to be my father."

"Do you know who I am?" the private asked quickly. The girl shook her head.

"Happy day," the soldier exclaimed as he raced out the door.

474 The hometown boy arrived back from the Academy, proud of his new uniform. He walked into a restaurant where several high school girls sat sipping cokes. "Hi," he said casually. "I'm a big West Pointer now.";

One of the girls looked at him disdainfully. "What do we care if you're an Irish Setter!"

---

475 The general's aide called in a dense, but uppity private and said, "Tomorrow, there'll be some high-ranking officers here for dinner. Your job is to stand at the door and call the guests' names as they enter."

"I'm for that," said the uppity private. "But who'll keep me from being court-martialed?"

MINISTERS, ADMIRERS

476 A young single minister gave this reason for resigning his first pastorate: "There were fourteen girls and three widows all trying to marry me."

"But don't you know there's safety in Numbers," someone reminded.

"That's not for me. I escaped in Exodus."

---

477 George Ade, a humorist, once stayed at a hotel in Indiana where a ministerial conference was being held. In the dining room, Ade found himself the only lay person. He told a friend later, "I felt like a lion in a den of Daniels."

MINISTERS, ANNOUNCEMENTS

478 A line in the church bulletin of a Texas Baptist church said: "The pastor will be gone next Sunday and we will be having a day of singing and praise."

MINISTERS, APPRECIATION

479 A pastor stopped off on his vacation to see an old classmate who pastored a church in a small town. "And how has the world been treating you, since we left the seminary?"

"Very seldom!" replied the pastor sadly.

MINISTERS, CALLING

480 Two baby chicks were discussing the absence of their father. "Where's daddy gone?" chirped one.

"Into the ministry," said the other sadly.

"Oh, he must not have been much of a layman."

~~~~~~

481 Billy: "My pop's a doctor, so I can be sick for nothing."

Tommy: "Huh, that's no big deal. My pop's a preacher, so I can be good for nothing."

~~~~~~

482 Two young boys were playing detective when the minister walked up. "Who are you?" one lad asked gruffly.

"Sacred Agent 007," replied the preacher who kept on walking.

MINISTERS, CHILDREN

483 A pastor's small daughter was put to bed with the sniffles. "Mother, may I see Daddy?"

she pleaded.

"No, dear," the mother said. "This is Saturday night and daddy is studying for tomorrow."

A few moments later she asked again and got the same answer.

The third time, she said solemnly to her mother, "I'm a sick woman, and I must see my minister at once."

MINISTERS, CHURCH MEMBERS

484 A minister discovered shortly before a church social on the parsonage lawn that his wife had forgotten to invite a certain touchy member. Quickly, he telephoned her an invitation.

"Too late," she snapped. "I've already prayed for rain!"

---

485 A minister wrote a letter of appreciation to be copied and mailed to members of his church. It read:

"My dear friends:

I will not use formality, and address you as ladies and gentlemen, because I know you so well..."

MINISTERS, EDUCATION

486 A fine preacher named Tweedle
Said as he refused a degree
"It's tough enough being Tweedle,
Without being Tweedle, D.D."

MINISTERS, FELLOWSHIP

487 Four ministers of different denominations frequently met for fellowship. One day they decided to help one another by confessing sins while the others listened sympathetically.

The Episcopalian rector began by admitting his pet sin was drinking. "I take too many nips from the bottle," he said.

The Methodist pastor said his sin was gambling. "When I'm on vacation, I play the slots," he admitted. "Please pray for me that I can break my gambling habit."

The Presbyterian confessed that he smoked in secret. "I know it isn't good for my health. I'm also ashamed of myself for doing it."

Eyes turned toward the Baptist. When he didn't speak up, the Methodist said. "Tell us yours, brother. Remember this is a gentleman's agreement. Or don't you have a secret sin?"

"I have one, but I don't think you'd like to hear it," said the Baptist.

"Yes, we would," chorused the other three. "We insist."

"Well, if you insist, then prepare yourself. My sin is gossip and I can hardly wait to get to a telephone."

MINISTERS, POLITICS

488 A Baptist seminary professor says there are four stages of progress up the ecclesiastical ladder: Yard dog, house dog, lap dog and big dog.

MINISTERS, PRAYER

489 A young minister had just published his first book and was filled with visions of greatness. He was still in the "clouds" when he entered the pulpit on Sunday morning and began his prayer, "O Thou who hast also written a book..."

490 A young minister came to a rural church as a candidate for pastor. He got carried away in his eloquence as he prayed, "And may the one who comes to minister to this flock be filled with veal and zigor."

491 A Methodist minister named Crow was attending a conference in Dallas, Texas. The presiding bishop got mixed up in asking Rev. Crow to lead in prayer and said, "Brother Pray, would you please crow for us."

MINISTERS, SALARIES

492 Woodrow Wilson grew up in a Presbyterian parsonage. His father was thin and gaunt and traveled about in a buggy pulled by a sleek horse.

The future president was asked by a man, "Why is your father so thin while his horse is so fat?"

Young Woodrow replied, "Perhaps it's because father feeds the horse and the congregation feeds father."

493 A Texas preacher was paid from offerings which church members put in a box at the church door. When a blizzard came, he didn't get any pay. One year there were four blizzard Sundays and his funds dropped perilously low. Finally on the fourth Tuesday he saw a member wading through the deep snow. His pulse quickened when he saw it was the church treasurer.

The treasurer finally reached the parsonage and asked, "Pastor, could you give me the address of that Gospel radio program that comes on at nine each Sunday morning? They inspired me during the blizzard and I'd like to send them a few dollars."

494 A lawyer's son and a pastor's son, both age six, were talking. Said the lawyer's boy, "My daddy talks to people for an hour and they pay him $100."

"Huh, that's nothing," said the preacher's kid. "My dad only talks for half an hour and it takes twelve men to carry all the money to him."

495 A pioneer Methodist circuit rider received only a little money from his four small congregations, hardly enough to feed himself and his horse. At one church they always told him, "Thank you, brother. You'll get your reward in the resurrection."

After being told this several times, the

preacher replied, "Yes, brothers and sisters, I know I'll get my reward in the resurrection, but my old horse won't have any resurrection and he'd appreciate something to eat now."

MINISTERS, SERMONS

496 An Irish preacher was in the habit of speaking critically of English preachers. He was invited to London to preach and cautioned to hold his tongue. But as he was preaching on the Lord's Supper he began giving the disciples' responses to Jesus' declaration that one would betray Him. Said the Irishman, "One by one the disciples said, 'Is it I?' Finally the Lord looked at Judas and Judas said, 'I say, Old Chap, is it I?'"

497 "At the close of my Sunday sermon," announced the pastor to the minister's conference, "there was a great awakening."

498 An Indian came to hear a famous preacher. Afterwards a member of the church asked the Indian his impression. Pronounced the Indian: "Big wind, loud thunder, no rain."

499 A church secretary in Illinois, in preparing the bulletin announcement about a guest minister, typed, "In the absence of the pastor, Mr. Hill will fell the pulpit."

500 The young pastor's sermons grew longer and longer, drier and drier, wordier and wordier. Attendance dropped so much that he scolded the people for not attending regularly. "I've done my best to follow Peter's advice as given in II Peter 2:2. I've sought to feed them the milk of the Word."

"Pastor," a deacon said, "I think the people prefer it condensed."

501 The minister was droning on when he noticed a man asleep in the congregation. He raised his voice and stamped his foot but did not wake the man up. Finally he called to a deacon. "Please wake that brother up."

The deacon replied, "You wake him up, preacher. You were the one who put him to sleep."

502 The fiery minister was waxing eloquent about the judgment day. "Thunder will boom. Lightning will flash. Flames will shoot from the sky. Floods, tornadoes, hurricanes and earthquakes will tear the world apart."

"Mommy," piped seven-year-old Billy. "Will I get out of school?"

503 A long-winded revivalist, preaching in a West Texas church, had been orating for more than an hour. His only pauses were to gulp a drink from a glass of water. Finally, during a pause for a drink, an aged farmer leaned toward his neighbor in the pew and whispered loudly, "First time I ever saw a windmill run by water."

504 A preacher had been tiring his audience for an hour about the terrible condition of the world and how he expected judgment soon to come. Finally, he howled, "What would you say, dear friends, if all the rivers in our great land dried up?"

A tired voice grumbled out loud, "I'd say, 'Go thou and do likewise.' "

505 Three preachers were talking about people looking at their watches during sermons. One said, "That doesn't bother me. It's when they start shaking them that I get aggravated."

"I can take the watch shaking," said another, "but I can't stand it when they start pulling out pocket and purse calendars."

"I can even take that," said the third. "I only get bothered when somebody gets up and asks, 'Who do you think you are? A Joshua, trying to make time stand still?' "

506 A Nebraska preacher announced his sermon in the church bulletin: "Next Sunday at 11 a.m.: 'Pearls Before Swine.' We should like to see you here."

507 A new seminary graduate appeared before a big church and preached a trial sermon. Later in the week he met one of his old professors who asked him how his sermon went. "Do you mean the one I was going to give" he asked, "or the one I did give, or the one I preached so eloquently while driving home?"

508 A young preacher, fresh out of seminary, was asked to deliver the sermon at a breakfast for area pastors. Afterwards an old preacher said, "Young man, your sermon was like the peace and mercy of God."

The young cleric smiled at what he thought was a compliment. Then he asked, "In what way was my sermon like the peace and mercy of God?"

"It was like the peace of God in that it passed all understanding. It was like His mercy in that I thought it would endure forever."

509 In a Nebraska community several members of the local Catholic church sat on their porches and listened to a strong-voiced evangelist preach in a nearby tent. They were quite impressed with the length of the sermons, since their priest spoke only a few minutes following each Sunday morning mass. Later one of the Catholics asked the priest why.

"Father," he said, "how is it that the Protestant preacher talked for an hour or more, while you never speak to us more than 20 minutes on Sunday morning?"

The priest looked down the road at the tent and replied, "Well, it's my opinion that if you can't knock a man down in 20 minutes, you'll never do it in an hour."

---

510 A pastor came into his pulpit on Sunday morning with a large band-aid on his chin. Before reading his text, he explained his injury. "I had my mind on my sermon this morning and cut my chin while shaving."

After the benediction that concluded the long sermon, a member said, "He should have kept his mind on his chin and cut his sermon."

---

511 A minister gave an unusual sermon one day using a peanut to make several points about the wisdom of God in nature. One of the members greeted him at the door and said, "Very interesting, Reverend. We learned a lot today from a nut."

---

512 A boy attended a Baptist church for the first time. At the end of the service, the minister asked him how he liked the service.

"The music was super," the boy said, "but you should shorten the commercial."

---

513 A pastor always preached 28 minutes, almost to the second. But one morning he ran on for over an hour. A deacon asked him about it and he blushed. "When I start," he said, "I always put a certain brand of cough drop in my mouth. It takes exactly 28 minutes to melt. This morning I made a mistake and put in my spare collar button."

514 The church janitor had been putting down new carpet around the pulpit platform and by mistake left several tacks scattered on top of the pulpit. The minister discovered this and said, "Now what do you think would happen to me if I should come up here Sunday morning and put my hand down on one of these tacks?"

The janitor couldn't hide his grin. "I reckon, pastor, that would be one point you wouldn't linger on for long."

515 One pastor's sermons got longer and longer. Finally they decided to change one letter in his title. Instead of "Reverend," they called him "Neverend."

516 All preachers should keep in mind the maxim: The mind cannot retain what the seat cannot endure.

517 A little boy asked his pastor, "When are you going to preach against floating kidneys?"

"What do you mean, sonny," the preacher asked.

"Well, last Sunday, you talked about loose livers."

MINISTERS, VISITATION

518 A new minister was getting acquainted with his people. He knocked on the front door of a newly married couple's home. "Is that you, Angel?" the young wife called.

"Not exactly," the pastor replied, "but I'm from the same office."

---

519 Little Jimmy ran into the house squealing with excitement. "Hey, Dad! Jerry and I caught a toad. We smashed and squished him until — " Suddenly he noticed the minister sitting at the table drinking coffee. "Until," Jimmy concluded solemnly, "God called him home."

---

520 A small boy came running to his mother. "Mamma, I've got a real bad tummy ache."

"That's because it's empty. You were out playing when we were eating dinner. Now come and get something to eat."

After Johnny ate, the minister dropped by. The boy's mother was in the kitchen when Johnny opened the door and asked, "How're ya doin', Brother Bill?"

"Right now I've got a terrible headache."

"That's cause it's empty. Mama says you'll feel better when you get something in it."

521 A minister habitually told his congregation that if anyone needed a pastoral visit to drop a note in the offering plate. One evening after services he discovered a note that said: "I am one of your loneliest members and heaviest contributors. May I have a visit tomorrow evening?" It was signed by his wife.

522 A kindly minister noticed a little boy straining on tiptoe to reach a doorbell. The minister finally walked up on the porch and pushed the button for the boy. The boy grinned when footsteps were heard from inside. Then suddenly he ran down the steps and squealed, "Run, Mister, here comes the lady."

MINISTERS, WISDOM

523 Peter Cartright, the pioneer circuit-riding Methodist preacher, met his share of ridicule. Once when returning from a circuit trip, he was met by several jaunty young men. As he tied his horse to the hitching rack, one said in mock solemnity, "Did you come back for the funeral, Reverend?"

"Whose funeral?" asked Cartright, showing concern.

"Haven't you heard? The devil is dead!"

"Oh, is that so?" Cartright replied in mock sadness. Then he reached in his pocket and handed their spokesman a quarter.

"What's this for?" the leader asked.

"For you and your friends. My religion has always taught me to be kind to orphans."

MINISTERS, WIVES

524 A former pastor and his wife attended the homecoming celebration of his old church. The new minister greeted the former minister graciously. "Very happy to meet you," he said, "And is this your most charming wife?"

"This," replied the former pastor in a stern voice, "is my only wife."

---

525 When the Southern Baptist Convention met in Memphis, Tennessee, a pastor from another state was asked to speak on a local religious radio program. A choral group of seminary students was asked to sing just before the guest minister's message. Just before the students came to sing, the visitor asked to make a dedication. "I should like to dedicate this song to the one who has stood by my side throughout my ministry, my beloved wife," he said.

The students then came and delivered the song they had rehearsed out of the minister's earshot, "Wandering Child, Please Come Home."

MINISTERS, WORK

526 A man saw his pastor walking along the street a block ahead of him. Suddenly the minister dropped from view. Hurrying up, the man saw that the preacher had dropped into an open manhole in the street. He ran to the nearby

fire station and shouted, "Bring the rescue
truck, quick. My preacher has fallen into a
manhole."

"Relax," said a fireman as he moved a
checker. "This is only Thursday. You won't need
him until Sunday."

527 A minister faced with a mountain of
tasks, remarked, "I'm like the circus elephant
that fell down and said, 'I don't know what
part of me to get up first.'"

MISCUES

528 An Arizona senator once referred to the
U.S. Military high command as "The Joint
Thiefs of Chaff." A Nebraska senator flubbed
and called them the "Chief Joints of Stiff."

529 A weather forecaster got confused and
predicted, "Rowdy followed by clain."

530 An international incident was almost
created by the American delegate to the United
Nations. He pleaded with the Jews and Arabs
to "settle their differences like Christians."

MISERS

531 When desperately ill, the town skinflint
pledged to give $5,000 to the hospital drive if he
recovered. He did recover, but failed to keep his

word and kept avoiding the doctor to whom he had made the pledge. Finally the doctor in charge of the drive cornered the tightwad on the street. "I need to collect your pledge," the doctor said. "I remember you promised to give $5,000 if you recovered your health."

"I did?" the old miser said in mock amazement. "I must have really been sick, then."

532 The town tightwad lost a hundred dollar bill. It was discovered by an honest man who advertised that he had found a bill and whoever named the denomination could have it.

The miser didn't take a newspaper and happened to hear about the ad secondhand three days later. He rushed over to the honest man's house and asked, "Was it a hundred dollar bill?"

"Yes," the finder said, "and since you know the denomination, here is your bill."

The miser took it and stood there as if waiting for something else. "Is everything all right?" the finder asked.

"That's my bill all right, but you've had it three days. Shouldn't I have some interest coming?"

533 The local penny-pincher was shopping and came to the egg counter. "What's the price of your cracked eggs?" she asked a nearby clerk.

"They're real cheap," the clerk assured. "Twenty-five cents a dozen."

"Good," the customer said. "Please crack me two dozen."

⸻

534 The community misers looked out their dining room window as they were eating dinner and saw a couple whom they knew coming toward their house. "Oh, oh," the woman wailed. "Here comes the Smiths and I'll bet they haven't eaten yet."

"Hurry, then," shouted her husband. "Let's get the toothpicks and get out on the porch."

MISSIONS

535 A minister was exhorting his flock to support foreign missionaries. One man loudly objected, "I don't approve of foreign missions."

"But surely," the minister countered, "you know the Bible tells us to feed the hungry?"

"Maybe so," the cheapskate said, "but can't we find something cheaper than missionaries to feed 'em?"

MISUNDERSTANDING

536 The society matron listened carefully to her doctor's advice. "Madam," he said, "you need to bathe frequently, get plenty of fresh air and dress in warm clothing."

Upon arriving home she told her husband, "Doctor Jones said I must take a trip to Hawaii, get a room at an exclusive dude ranch and buy myself a full-length mink coat."

MONEY

537 Their bank account's insufficient
By one feminine flaw;
He's fast on the deposit;
She's quicker on the draw.

---

538 Weary husband paying bills: "Looks like we'll have to rob Peter to pay Paul so we can stand pat."

---

539 The housewife worked for two hours trying to balance their joint checking account. When her husband arrived home she handed him a neatly typed sheet with items and amounts in neat columns and showing an exact balance. He ran down the list until he came to one item reading, ESP: $43.49. "What's that you bought?" he asked.

"I didn't really buy anything," she smiled. "That means error some place."

---

540 A husband called to his wife who was sitting at the kitchen table one Saturday morning, paying bills. "Dr. Dawes on the radio said we're taller in the morning than in the evening," he reported. "Maybe that's why women wear high heels when they go out at night."

"I wouldn't know about that," she said, "but I have noticed we're shorter around the end of the month."

541 Two scientists were debating the possibility of life on the planet Uranus. "I'm sure there's no life there," said one. "It's never been listed on our phone bill."

542 The young husband looked at the new clothes his wife had just bought and began to lecture her on economy. "You just don't seem to understand that for us money doesn't grow on trees," he said.

"Okay, smarty," she replied. "I admit I'm a money spender, but try and name one other extravagance."

543 The young country bride was hesitant about asking her husband for money. "Frank, dear," she said meekly when he came home from work. "I've spent my house allowance. Would you lend me $20, but only give me half now?"

"Sure," the husband said, "but why only half now?"

"Well, then you'll owe me ten and I'll owe you ten and we'll be even, won't we?"

544 A reporter was interviewing a wealthy man. "To what do you credit your financial success?" he asked.

The rich man looked thoughtful. "I believe the just due should go to my wife."

"She loyally stood...?"

"Not that," the rich man interrupted, "I just wanted to see if there was any income she couldn't live beyond."

545 Extravagance: The way other people spend their money.

Budgeting: The way you spend your money.

546 Teacher: "Jerry, if your father earned $500 a week and gave your mother half, what would she have?"

"A heart attack for sure!"

547 "How's your new wife taking the loss of your fortune?" the lawyer asked his client.

"She's a real money grubber," he replied. "She's home sifting the ashes."

548 "My wife's begging me for pin money," a man told his buddy at the office.

"Give it to her," he said. "Don't be so cheap."

"You don't know my wife. She wants a pin with six diamonds in it."

549 "Did you know," said Lolly, "that some Eskimos use fish hooks for money?"

"Well, whatta ya think of that," replied Molly. "I wonder how the wives get the fish hooks out of the pockets while the husbands are asleep?"

"They should be able to do it," reasoned Lolly.

"It says here the nights are six months long up there now."

MONKEYS AND APES

550 An ape walked into a fast-food place and ordered a milkshake. He gave the manager a $10 bill for the dollar treat. The manager thought, "Apes don't know much about money," and handed back $2.00 in change.

Finally the manager's curiosity got the best of him and he said, "We don't have many apes come in here."

"The ape replied, "I can see why when you charge $8.00 for a dollar milkshake."

551 *"Monkeys and Men"*
"Three monkeys sat in a coconut tree
Discussing things as they're said to be:
Said one to the others, "Now listen you two,
There's a certain rumor that can't be true;
That man descended from our noble race;
Why, the very idea, it's a dire disgrace.
No monkey ever deserted his wife,
Starved her baby and ruined her life.
Another thing you'll never see,
A monk built a fence around a coconut tree,
Forbidding all the other monks a taste,
And letting the coconuts go to waste.
Another thing a monk won't do
Is get out at night and get on a stew,
And take a gun, club or knife,
And take some other monkey's life.
Yes, man descended, the ornery cuss,
But, brother, he didn't descend from us."

MOONSHINERS

552 A graduate student from a big university was writing his thesis on illegally-made alcohol. He decided to do some field research in the West Virginia mountains and stopped in a hamlet to seek information.

Spotting a tall, gangly youth in overalls, he asked, "Are there any illegal alcohol stills in operation around here?"

"Shore are," said the boy.

"Good. If you'll take me to see one, I'll give you five dollars."

"Will ya give me the five dollars now?" asked the boy.

"Why now?" queried the stranger.

"'Cause if I take ya to a still, ya ain't comin' back."

---

553 A young moonshiner was in court. "What's your name, son?" the judge asked.

"Joshua, Your Honor."

"Ah, ha," said the judge in a teasing way. "Are you the Joshua that made the sun stand still?"

"No, Your Honor, I'm the Joshua that the sheriff says made the moonshine still."

MOTELS

554 A traveling salesman from Georgia was driving to see a customer in northern Wisconsin and stopped at a motel that advertised "TV."

He checked in, went to his room, looked around, then called the manager. "Ya'll don't have a TV in my room. You have a sign out front that says you have TV."

"No, no, you don't understand," said the Swedish desk clerk. "That sign you saw means 'Tourists Velcome.'"

MOTHERHOOD

555 A perspiring woman boarded a city transit bus with 11 wiggly children from age 12 down to a baby. The driver smiled and said, "Are these all yours, or are you just taking the neighborhood kids on a picnic?"

"Mister," she replied, "They're all mine, and as I keep telling my husband, it sure isn't any picnic."

556 A woman, driving an old station wagon loaded with children, almost hit a traffic policeman.

"Madam, don't you know when to stop?" the officer said, pointing his finger at a sign.

The woman's face froze. "Half of 'em belong to my sister," she said frigidly.

557 A harried mother was traveling on a Greyhound bus with two attractive children. "Such lovely children," the woman across the aisle said. "I'd give a dozen years of my life just to have them."

"That," said the tired mother, "is just about what they have cost me."

558 Difference between a barber and a mother: One has razors to shave and the other has shavers to raise.

559 A Boy Scout troop arrived at summer camp. The scoutmaster made an equipment inspection and discovered one boy had brought two heavy quilts and an umbrella. "Why did you bring all this stuff?" he asked.

"Sir," the young scout blurted, "didn't you ever have a mother?"

560 A small boy ran in to where his mother was putting away dishes and asked the question she had long dreaded: "Mama, where did I come from?"

The mother turned pale and leaned against the sink to support herself. Finally she managed to speak and began a long detailed explanation of how children are conceived and born. When she finally stopped, the little boy wiped his nose and said, "Mama, I don't care about all that stuff. All I wanted to know was where I come from. Harold, the new boy in my class, comes from Houston, Texas and he asked where did I come from."

561 A little daughter had been very difficult all day. While tucking her in, her mother said, "Dear, I do hope you'll be a better girl tomorrow and not make everybody so miserable with your nasty temper."

The daughter listened quietly, then asked, "Mommy, why is it always my temper, but when you get angry it's your nerves?"

MOTHERS-IN-LAW

562 "Henry," said the puzzled wife, "I've got a letter from mother saying she isn't coming to visit us because she thinks we don't want her. Didn't I ask you to write and invite her to come at her own convenience?"

"Yes, sweetie, but I had trouble spelling that word 'convenience,' so I put 'risk' instead."

563 A fellow was driving his car along a curvy, crooked highway with his wife and mother-in-law. Both women kept telling him how fast to drive, when to slow, when to pass, etc. Finally he pulled off the road and snapped at his wife, "Okay, Helen, make up your mind. Who's driving this car, you or your mother?"

564 The extreme penalty for bigamy is two mothers-in-law.

MOUNTAIN CLIMBING

565 Max looked up at the steep icy mountainside. "I can't," he said.

His companions kept begging him to climb the mountain with them. But he refused to move. "I'm against mountain climbing," he declared.

Now they call him "Anti-climb-Max."

~~~~~~

566 Several Nepalese mountain climbers from the Himalayan Mountains of Asia were visiting the United States to recruit tourists. The manager of the travel agency which had arranged for their visit took them to the top of the Sears skyscraper in Chicago. "Isn't this a wonderful view?" their American host gushed.

"It's okay, I guess," said one of the Nepalese. "But if we were home and climbing this, we'd still be in the basement."

MOVIES

567 A man rushed into a movie theater where an "R" rated film was on. "How late am I?" he asked an usher.

The usher looked at his watch. "Only 30 minutes. But don't worry, you've missed the worst of it."

MUSICIANS

568 Conceited singer to critic: "Did you hear how my voice filled the building?"

Music critic: "Yes, I did. I noticed some people leaving to make room for it."

~~~~~~

569 A young girl was practicing her violin lesson while the next door neighbor's hound dog howled pitifully. The neighbor took all he could and finally came over to talk to Sandra's parents. "Please, can't the girl play something the dog doesn't know?"

---

570 Collector for piano company: "Mr. Hawkins, you're five payments behind on your new piano."

Hawkins: "Am I? Doesn't your company advertise that you 'pay as you play'?"

Collector; "Yes, but what's that got to do with your delinquency?"

Hawkins: "I play poorly."

---

571 "My daughter can play the piano by ear," said one proud mother.

"That's nothing," said the other mother. "My son's a country singer. He can sing through his nose by ear."

---

572 Musician to physician: "Doc, will you fix me up so I can play my violin in the symphony for the big concert?"

Physician: "Only if you promise to pay my bill. Otherwise, I'll have you playing a harp."

---

573 A long-haired musician was observed lying in a coffin. He was quite alive and busily erasing music scores he had written the day before. When asked, "What are you doing?" he replied, "Decomposing."

574 Then there was the bald-headed musician whose toupee fell over the mouth of his horn. He blew his top all night.

575 A wealthy society woman hired a famous concert pianist to accompany her in singing for a charity dinner. After the first solo, she noticed that the pianist was frowning. "What's wrong?" she asked. "Don't you like my voice?"

"Madam," he replied, "I have played on the white keys and I have played on the black keys, but you sing in the cracks."

576 There was a quartet named the "Four Fish Brothers": first tuna, second tuna, barracuda and base.

577 A man knocked on the door. "Who are you?" the lady of the house asked.

"Jones, the piano tuner."

"But I didn't send for you," she protested.

"No, but the couple in the apartment upstairs did."

NAMES

578 A Missouri Pacific Railroad agent was seeking advice about a train station in a new Arkansas community. A resident told him, "You kin set hit hyar, air you ken set hit thar." The town was later named Kensett, Arkansas.

***

579 Years ago an engineer taking a train from
Pine Bluff, Arkansas to New Orleans became
confused in the fog. He thought he was near
Eudora, Arkansas which is close to the
Louisiana border. Spotting a huddle of houses
along one side of the track, he stopped the train
and hollered, "Is this, Eudora?"

A woman's voice answered back, "Naw, this
is Jenny."

And that's how the town of Jenny got its
name.

***

580 Years ago there were few signs for
travelers on a road running through northwest
Georgia to Alabama. When a cluster of houses
were erected along the road near the Alabama
and Tennessee borders, travelers would stop
and ask residents where they were. People
would answer, "Ya're plum out of Tennessee and
nelly out of Georgia." That's how the little
settlement called "Plum Nelly" got its name.

***

581 Who's the brother of Snow White? Egg
White. Get the yolk?

***

582 An Apache Indian chief named Shortcake
died. The young braves argued among
themselves as to who would have the honor of
burying Chief Shortcake. They agreed to settle

the matter with a wrestling duel. The brave who won was named Straw. He shouted in triumph, "Straw bury Shortcake."

NATIONS

583 *Famous Firsts:*

Where was the first doughnut made? Greece.
The first Thanksgiving observed? Turkey.
The first temper tantrum? Ire-land.
The first disease? Germ-any.
The first ice cream? Ice-land.
The first crab grass? Green-land.
The first foot race? I-ran.
The first pig used in an experiment? Guinea.
The first crying over spilled milk? Wales.
The first whipping? Switzer(switcher)-land.
The first famine? Hungary.
The first dieting? Bulg-aria.

584 An admirer of Lincoln during the Civil War saw the President from a distance and shouted, "Mr. President, I'm from up in New York State where we believe that God Almighty and Abraham Lincoln are going to save this country."

Lincoln nodded his head in recognition, then said, "My friend, you are half right."

NEIGHBORS

585 An old farmer came in to the county seat and asked a lawyer to file a slander suit against a neighbor. "What did he do?" the lawyer asked.

"Called me a hippopotamus," the farmer snorted.

"When did he do this?"

"Nine years ago."

"Why have you waited all this time?"

"Cause I never saw a hippopotamus til last week when my city son took me to the zoo."

586 Jenkins barely managed to contain his anger when his neighbor called at four a.m. "Your dog is barking so loudly I can't sleep," the neighbor growled and then hung up.

The next morning at exactly four, Jenkins called the neighbor and said, "I haven't got a dog." Then he hung up.

587 Bill's friend dropped by his apartment and asked, "How does your new short-wave radio work?"

"Just beautiful," Bill said. "I tuned in Nigeria at four o'clock this morning. Came in loud and clear."

"And what else did you get?" the friend asked.

"Brooms, milk bottles, old shoes and a tea kettle."

NEWSPAPERS

588 An editor was schooling his reporters on writing headlines. "I want each of you to make a headline in two words which will really sell newspapers."

The two-word winning headlines included: "Castro Shaves," "Iceland Melts" and "Pope Elopes," which was voted the winner.

589 A cub reporter was assigned to cover an important wedding where the son of the Republican mayor in the largest town was to marry the daughter of the Democratic congressman in that district. The editor waited for the phone call for two hours after time for the ceremony passed. Finally the cub came strolling in. "Where's the story?" the editor growled.

The cub sadly shook his head. "No story. The bride's father wouldn't let her show up."

590 A late reporter came rushing up to a house where a murder had been committed. As he started through the doorway, a policeman stepped out. "Get lost, buddy. You can't come in here."

"But I've got to get in. I've been assigned to do the murder."

"Well, you're too late," the cop said. "Someone has already done it."

591 A new reporter covered his first murder trial for the county seat paper. He wrote a double headline: "DEFENDANT ESCAPES GALLOWS: JURY HUNG."

592 A feature writer from a big city paper was traveling to the scene of a big story and stopped on the way to say hello to an old college chum who edited a small-town weekly.

"How do you manage to keep up your circulation in a town where everyone already knows what everybody else is doing?"

The small-town editor smiled. "They read my paper to see who's been caught."

593 A reporter for a big city daily was out digging up human interest stories in the rural region. He spotted a whittler on the parking bench in front of the courthouse and asked, "Lived here all your life, grandpa?"

"Don't rightly know, young feller," the old man said. "They hain't had my funeral yet."

594 A reporter called in sick. About 11 o'clock the managing editor yelled to his assistant. "Jones is sick. Go dig someone up to write the obituaries."

595 An editor received a phone call from a controversial politician. "You say our paper ran your obituary yesterday? Yes. Yes. Er, uh, tell me where you're calling from."

596 A newspaper corrected a line that read:

"The mayor talked about defectives on the police force." The corrected copy read: "The mayor balked about detectives on the police force."

NURSES

597 A fellow had been operated on and had just been taken back to his room. When he opened his eyes, he noticed that the window blinds were closed. He called the nurse and asked why.

"There's a fire across the street," she explained. "I closed the blinds because when you awakened I didn't want you to think the operation had failed."

598 A small girl was being prepared for her shot to enter school for the new year. The nurse asked, "Which arm do you want the shot in this time?"

She immediately answered, "Mama's."

599 The doctor assigned a pretty new nurse to private rooms. "Because," he said, "she's too cute for wards."

OBESITY

600 A pompous, overweight white businessman met a distinguished Indian chief in the west. "Heap big chief," the Indian said, thumping on his chest."

The fat white man pounded his chest. "And me heap big businessman."

"No," declared the Indian. You just big heap."

OPPOSITION

601 Abraham Lincoln told this story when his entire Cabinet stood against him, excepting one member:

"An Illinois revival preacher asked his congregation, 'All on the Lord's side, please stand to your feet.' The whole audience arose, except for a sleeping drunk. Then the preacher asked, 'Will those on the Devil's side now stand?'

"The drunk suddenly awoke, jumped to his feet, and said, 'I didn't exactly understand your question, but I'll stand by you, parson, to the end. Seems to me we're in a hopeless minority.' "

OPTICIAN

602 An optician fell into his lens grinder and made a spectacle of himself.

PARENTHOOD

603 A mother, who had been raised in the country, was scolding her educated daughter for her careless hairdo. "You city girls don't care how you look. Your hair looks worse than a mop."

To which the daughter inquired innocently, "What's a mop?"

604 The father of four cleared the room of toys and chuckled to the minister who was visiting. "Since I've been married, I've learned what the Apostle Paul meant when he said, 'When I became a man, I put away childish things.' "

605 A father from the old school says he has learned how to tell which of his three boys is the culprit when trouble appears and none is willing to tell on a brother.

"I put them to bed," he said, "without supper or TV. Next morning I take to the woodshed the one with a black eye."

606 A love-struck 17-year-old was begging his father to sign for his marriage license. "Don't worry about me making a living, Dad. Two can live as cheaply as one!"

"How well I know," sighed the father. "Your mother and I have lived as cheaply as you for some time."

607 A critical neighbor was speaking of the spoiled young man who at 27 still lived with his parents. "He went to college and received a B.A., but his M.A. and his P.A. still support him."

PARKING

608 A tired motorist parked his car in a no-parking space and left this message on the windshield: "I have circled this block 25 times. I have an appointment I must keep or lose my job. Forgive me my trespasses."

Upon returning he found attached to a ticket this note: "If I don't give you a ticket, I could lose my job. Lead me not into temptation."

PARTNERSHIP

609 A short man and a tall man went into the moving business. One day they were called to move a piano from the third to the first floor of a building. They went up to the third floor and decided they could maneuver the piano through the third floor window, use an improvised pulley to drop the piano to the first floor, then swing the piano through a window into the desired room.

The tall man said to his short partner, "I'll push the piano out of the third floor window. You go down to the first floor, hold the rope, and let the piano down slowly."

The tall man pushed the piano out of the window on to the pulley. The little man shot upward and hit the roof. The piano fell and broke into splinters and the little man fell into the debris.

The tall man rushed downstairs and found his partner unconscious. "Joe, speak to me," he begged. Finally the little man awakened and said, "Why should I? I went by you twice and you didn't speak to me."

PATRIOTISM

610 Teacher to fifth-grader: "Johnny, what famous speech did Paul Revere say when he finished his ride?"

Johnny: "Whoa, Nellie!"

PEDESTRIANS

611 Rhyme for pedestrian safety:

Bill looked.
Joe didn't.
Bill is.
Joe isn't.

※※※※※※※※※※※※※※※※※※※※※※※※※

612 A driver shrieked to a stop on a country road just inches from an elderly man crossing the road. "Why don't you look when you cross the road?" the driver yelled.

"Ha!" replied the old timer. "I oughta have rightaway. I've made more payments on this road than you have on your car."

※※※※※※※※※※※※※※※※※※※※※※※※※

613 A stranger observed a rangy, wooly-haired country boy running across the road while cars coming from both directions shrieked to a stop. "You'd think he'd get run over," the stranger said. "Instead the cars all stop for him. I don't get it."

"Look at the box he's carrying," said the stranger's city friend. "He always carries a box marked DYNAMITE in red letters and nobody has hit him yet."

PHOBIAS

614 You may have a phobia and not know it. Check this list:

Skopophobia — fear of spies.

Tapheophobia — fear of being buried alive.

Chronophobia — impulsive desire to smash clocks.

Amathophobia — fear of dust.

Uranophobia — fear of going to Heaven.
Triakaidekaphobia — fear of the number 13.

PHOTOGRAPHERS

615 At a country music festival, these printed instructions were given to the press photographers: "Do not photograph entertainers as they are performing before the audience. Shoot them as they approach the stage."

PILOTS

616 Supersonic jet pilot: "We're getting near the airport."

Co-pilot: "What makes you think that?"

Pilot: "The control tower just radioed that we're breaking more windows."

617 A passenger looked out of the plane window and saw the left wing burning. He looked out the other side and saw the right wing burning. Then he saw the pilot leap with a parachute.

"I'm going for help," the pilot yelled.

618 A Japanese and an American businessman were having lunch in Tokyo. "I was a Kamikaze suicide flier during the war," said the Japanese who was named Chow Mein.

"Now how could that be?" joshed the American. "You wouldn't be here if you were. That was a suicide squad."

"Oh, they call me Chicken Chow Mein."

PLAYS

619 A tired husband, dragged to a play by his wife, was seated behind a woman wearing an indescribable hat. Finally the woman turned around and said, "Is my hat restricting your view, sir?"

"Keep it on, lady," the husband said. "It's funnier than the play."

POLITICS

620 Said one politician to another: "Shall we carry on this campaign without any mud-slinging?"

"Splendid idea," the other said. "Here's what we can do. If you will refrain from telling any lies about the Republican Party, I will promise not to tell the truth about the Democratic Party."

621 A politician was barnstorming for votes in a small town. Seeking to get off to a good start with his audience, he began thus:

"My great-grandfather was a Roman Catholic (silence), but great-grandmother was an Episcopalian (more silence). Grandfather followed neither faith, but chose to become a Baptist (a few claps). Grandmother showed her independence by becoming a Lutheran (a few more claps). But my mother and father were Methodists (loud applause) and I've always dutifully followed my parents."

622 Said the director of the party's political show to the aspiring young candidate for alderman, "Smile, smile. You're on candidate camera!"

623 A would-be political candidate wanted to know his chances for election and hired a pollster to sample public opinion. Two weeks later the pollster reported: "I think 95% of the people are for you. Funny thing, though, I kept meeting only the other five percent."

624 A politician campaigning for office suddenly reversed an important plank in his platform. He was congratulated by a friend who had disagreed with him. "I'm glad you've seen the light," the friend said.

"Seen the light, nothing! I felt the heat!"

625 A politician who was prevented by law from succeeding himself proposed to run his wife. Complained his opponent, "He's skirting the law."

626 A political candidate was making a speech when suddenly a heckler began shouting, "Liar! Liar!"

Finally the candidate stopped and pointed to the disturber. "If you, sir, will be kind enough to give me your name instead of your calling, I will be happy to meet with you later."

627 A politician running for office announced the results of a poll on a squirrel hunting issue coming before the voters. In summing up, the candidate said, "Some of my friends are for it and some are against it."

When asked, "Where do you stand?" he replied, "I'm with my friends."

628 Said a politician: "I'm a vegetarian. I go for straw votes and grass roots."

629 A candidate running for public office is much like a quarterback calling a play. A lot depends on the line.

630 Years ago a crowd gathered to watch a southerner who was condemned to be hanged for murder. Under state law the condemned man was permitted five minutes to say whatever last words he wished. When his time came, the man said, "I haven't got anything to say. Go ahead with the hanging."

A man among the watchers pushed his way through the crowd. "If he doesn't want those five minutes, sheriff, I'll take them. I'm running for Congress."

631 Two politicians were running against each other for Congress. One was asked the difference between a misfortune and a calamity and replied: "If my honorable opponent fell into the river, that would be a misfortune, but if somebody dragged him out, that would be a calamity."

632 An Irish politician asked an elderly lady, one of his staunch supporters, "And what did your late husband die of?"

"Sure, and he died of a Tuesday," she replied. "I'll never forget the day."

633 What is the difference between a western gunfighter and an impetuous politician? The gunfighter shoots from the hip. The politician hoots from the lip.

634 With Congress, every time they make a joke it's a law. And every time they make a law it's a joke.

635 A politician on the campaign trail met a one-armed veteran. "I'm running for Congress," said the candidate. "Hope I can count on your vote."

The man looked down at his empty sleeve. "Well, I'm not sure I can vote for you."

"Of course you can," said the politician. "It only takes one arm to pull that lever on the voting machine."

"I know that," said the vet, "but how would I hold my nose."

〰〰〰〰〰〰〰〰〰〰〰〰〰〰〰〰〰〰〰〰〰〰

636 Abraham Lincoln once ran against the famous Methodist evangelist, Peter Cartright, for a seat in Congress. Lincoln heard that Cartright was combining politicking and preaching and decided to visit one of his meetings. During the meeting Cartright asked, "All those who want to go to heaven, now, please stand up." A large majority stood. Then he asked, "Those who don't want to go to hell, please stand up." Everyone stood except Lincoln.

"And where do you want to go, Mr. Lincoln?" Cartright asked.

"Only to Congress," Lincoln replied.

〰〰〰〰〰〰〰〰〰〰〰〰〰〰〰〰〰〰〰〰〰〰

637 A South American peasant was describing the exciting career of his uncle, a well-known revolutionary. "First, he ran for mayor and he made it. Then he ran for senator and made it. Then he ran for governor and made it. Then he ran for president and was elected. Then he ran for the airport — but he didn't make it."

〰〰〰〰〰〰〰〰〰〰〰〰〰〰〰〰〰〰〰〰〰〰

638 Politics is the most promising of all vocations: Promises, promises, promises,

promises....

***

639 One politician dedicated himself so many times that he came to feel like the cornerstone of a public building.

***

640 Said one politician of the man running against him: "My opponent is the kind of candidate who would cut down a redwood tree and then mount the stump for a speech on conservation."

***

641 "The office-holder I am trying to defeat," said the challenger, "is a 'me-too' candidate, running on a 'yes-but' platform, advised by a 'has-been' staff."

***

642 Said the standard-bearer of a major party: "I, like members of the opposite party, have grown up with them, worked with them, and would trust them with anything in the world — except public office."

***

643 "My opponent is like a chameleon lizard who tries to please everybody with a different color," said the aspirant for public office. "He turns red when placed on a red rug and brown when put on a brown rug. I fear that he will die a terrible death when placed on a Scotch plaid."

644 "I rose to speak," said the political candidate, "and one of my opponent's supporters threw a cowardly egg at me."

"And what is a cowardly egg?" a listener asked.

"One that hits you and runs."

POSTAL SERVICE

645 Postal authorities in Washington became concerned by reports that mail wasn't reaching the residents of a small, remote Ozark community. They called the newly-appointed postmaster to inquire the reason.

"Bag ain't full yet," he replied.

646 The ancient Incas of Peru did not use horses. They delivered messages by a series of runners who raced from post to post, much like the American Pony Express. This marked the first use of Inca racers (ink erasers).

POVERTY

647 A political candidate in Kansas said, "I was not born in a log cabin, like my opponent, but my family moved into one as soon as we could afford it."

648 Before the river bridge was built, Uncle Lem ran the ferry at Squirrel Tree Crossing.

The fare was 25 cents. One day Lige Parker asked to cross over, but he only had 23 cents. Uncle Lem chewed on this for awhile, then announced his decision: "If a feller ain't got but 23 cents, hit don't make no matter which side of the river he's on."

649 Farmer Pete Villines from Caddo Gap said he grew up so poor "that Mama sprinkled baking soda on me instead of talcum powder. Trouble was, ever' week or so I'd break out with a bad case of cookies."

PRAYER

650 A selfish man prayed:
"Lord, bless me and my wife,
Son John and his wife,
Us four and no more. Amen."

651 The hard-nosed vice-president called a poorly-paid employee into his office. "Smith, I've heard that you've been going over my head!"

Poor Jones murmured that he couldn't recall talking to the company president.

"That's not what I mean," the vice president declared. "Haven't you been praying for a raise?"

652 A father and his son were walking home after church, when the boy asked, "Daddy, why do they always say 'ah-men' when they finish praying. Why don't they ever say,'ah-women'?"

"It's an old custom, son," the father tried to explain. "It's like this — "

His son cut him short. "I get it. It's 'cause the songs have always been hymns."

---

653 Little girl's nightly prayer: "God bless Mommy, Daddy and baby sister. Amen, AM, FM, TV and VCR."

---

654 Presidential assistant Bill Moyers, formerly a Baptist minister, was giving thanks at a lunch with President Lyndon Johnson. Moyers' prayer was interrupted by the President, who said, "Speak up, Bill, I can't hear you."

Muttered Moyers: "I wasn't speaking to you, Mr. President."

---

655 Little Jenny was rushing to school. "Please, Lord, don't let me be late," she prayed anxiously as she heard the bell ringing. Just then she tripped and fell. As she got up and dusted herself off, she said in a hurt tone, "Well, I didn't ask for a push."

---

656 A Sunday school teacher asked a young miss in her class to define prayer. "Prayer," said the child, "is messages sent up at night and on Sundays when the rates are lower."

657 A young woman prayed, "Dear Lord, I'm not asking just for myself, but please give my mother a son-in-law. And if You don't mind, please let it be Harry Thornton."

658 A Baptist preacher prayed for "those who are sick of our church and congregation."

659 A boy from Pennsylvania got one phrase of the Lord's prayer mixed up. He intoned, "And lead us not into Penn Station."

PRESIDENTS

660 Will Rogers was a gifted imitator, and especially enjoyed imitating President Calvin Coolidge. On a radio broadcast, he began talking like Coolidge in a deadpan monotone. "It gives me great pleasure to report on the state of the nation. The nation is prosperous as a whole, but how much prosperity is there in a hole?"

PRIDE

661 Josh Billings said that most people are like eggs — too full of themselves to hold anything else.

662 Senator Charles Sumner of Massachusetts found President Lincoln polishing his boots. Amazed, the Senator said: "Why, Mr. President, do you black your own boots?"

Lincoln slapped the brush on leather briskly. "Well, whose boots did you think I'd black?"

PRISONERS

663 In Communist Cuba a factory night watchman spotted a worker going out with a wheelbarrow filled with trash. "Aha, I caught you," the watchman exclaimed as he proceeded to search the trash. He found nothing.

After this happened 31 more times, the watchman pleaded to the worker taking out trash. "I know you've been stealing something. Since I'm being sent to prison, I am no longer required to report you. Please tell me what it is?"

The worker kept pushing as he said, "Only wheelbarrows."

664 There was a prisoner whose troubles ran in streaks. First he had an abscessed tooth that had to be pulled. Next his appendix had to come out. Then came a growth on his arm. But when his foot was injured in an accident and had to be amputated, that was too much for the warden.

"You don't fool me, Smith," said the warden. "You're trying to escape piece by piece."

665 A social worker visiting a prison stopped to comfort a sad looking man listening to a transistor radio. "You must be without hope," she said. "How many more years must you serve?"

"That depends on the election, lady. The reports coming in aren't so good."

"Are you expecting the new governor to pardon you?"

"Not exactly. You see, I'm the warden."

666 "I'm a strong believer," the prisoner assured the chaplain.

"How's that?"

"I'm here because of my convictions."

667 The warden of a prison began feeling sorry for one of the prisoners who never had any relatives call on visitors' day. On other days the inmate seemed friendly and jovial enough but on visitors' day he always stayed in his cell looking lonely.

On visitors' day the warden called him into the office. "Joe," he said kindly, "don't you have any friends or family?"

"Sure, Warden," Joe replied happily, "they're all in here with me."

668 A good woman was visiting the inmates of a prison on Sunday afternoon. Coming up to one old convict, she asked, "And what is your name, sir?"

"684312," he said.

"That isn't your real name, is it?"

"Naw, lady, dat's only me pen name."

669 The police captain angrily confronted the new rookie cop. "You let the prisoner escape! Didn't I tell you to guard all exits?"

"Sir, I guarded every exit. He slipped through one of the entrances."

670 "Your name, please," demanded the judge, and your occupation and the charges against you."

"My name is Sparks," said the prisoner. "I'm an electrician, and I'm charged with battery."

The judge heard the case, then said, "Officer, put this man in a dry cell and conduct him there by a short circuit."

"I'm shocked," said the prisoner.

PROFESSORS

671 A student said of his history professor, "He's a real buried treasure. It was a sad day when they dug him up."

PROPOSAL

672 In years past Burma-Shave signs kept travelers alert. You had to read a series of signs to get the message. This mind-grabber took six signs:
 I Proposed
 To Ida
 Ida Refused
 I'da Won My Ida
 If I'da Used
 Burma-Shave.

673 Daughter: "Oh, mother, please tell me if I should accept Bill's proposal."

Mother: "Why don't you ask your father? He made a much smarter choice in marriage than I did."

674 A single woman came into her office and began passing out candy with blue ribbons. "What's the occasion?" someone asked.

She proudly lifted her hand to display the sparkling diamond. "It's a boy — six four and 190 pounds."

675 New clerk to bank president: "Sir, may I have permission to marry your daughter?"

President: "Er, uh."

Clerk (interrupting): "That is, if you have one."

676 Joe: "I'll never ask another woman to marry me so long as I live."

Fred: "Turned down again, eh?"

Joe: "No, this one accepted."

677 A fellow asked a man for his daughter's hand. "Are you sure you can support a family?" the man asked.

"No, sir, I'm not. But I was only planning on supporting your daughter. The rest of you will have to make it on your own."

PSYCHIATRISTS AND PSYCHOLOGISTS

678 Wife to psychiatrist: "My husband frightens me the way he blows smoke rings through his nose."

Psychiatrist: "That isn't unusual for smokers."

Wife: "But Bill doesn't smoke."

679 Said the troubled wife as the pastor entered and found her husband dangling a fishing lure into a bucket of water in the middle of the living room: "I'd take him to a psychiatrist, pastor, but we really need the fish."

680 A kangaroo visited a psychiatrist. "What's your problem?" the doctor asked.

"I haven't been feeling jumpy lately."

681 A wife confided to her family doctor, "I'm so upset. My Henry seems to be wandering in his mind."

"Don't let that worry you," assured the doctor. "I know Henry pretty well. He can't go far."

682 A woman complained to her therapist, "Doctor, it's awful. My husband thinks he's a refrigerator."

"I wouldn't worry," the doctor said, "so long as he isn't violent."

"Oh, the delusion doesn't bother me. But when he sleeps with his mouth open, the little light keeps me awake."

683 A mother took her young bully boy to a psychiatrist. "Does he feel insecure?" the doctor asked.

"That isn't the problem with him," she retorted. "It's the other kids in the neighborhood that feel insecure."

684 A policeman saw a psychiatrist toting a heavy couch down the street. "Moving, doc?" he asked cheerily.

"No. Just going on a house call."

685 A man got into the habit of kicking over his neighbor's garbage can when he left for work each morning. The neighbor thought at first it was a dog or a teenage vandal. Finally he caught the man and demanded an explanation.

"It's a compulsion," the can kicker said. "I can't keep from doing it."

Finally the man agreed to be treated in a mental institution. After several weeks he returned home and started the same old procedure again.

This time the neighbor was indignant. "Didn't the doctors help you?" he asked.

"Sure," the man said. "I don't feel embarrassed anymore."

---

686 A man came in to see a psychiatrist and said, "I'm afraid I've lost my memory. I need your help, Doctor."

The psychiatrist signalled to his nurse and said, "Quick, before I put him on the couch, give him a bill and have him pay in advance."

---

687 A wild-eyed fellow ran into a psychiatrist's office and began clapping his hands. "What's that for?" asked the doctor.

"That's to chase away the bears," he said.

"There aren't any bears in here."

"I know — I chased them all away."

---

688 A man came to a psychologist and complained of a weak memory.

"How long has this problem bothered you?" the psychologist asked.

"What problem?"

---

689 A man went to a therapist and identified himself as a sheep.

"How long have you been a sheep?" asked the doctor.

"Ever since I was a lamb," he replied.

PUBLIC OFFICE

690 A tourist came into a country town and asked around for the mayor. The first citizen exclaimed, "That jerk!"

The second citizen moaned, "That bum!"

The pollster received three more similar replies — crook, phony, nut — until meeting the mayor.

"Why did you run for this office?" the tourist asked.

"For the honor that goes with it," the mayor replied.

QUARRELS

691 A man and his wife were embroiled in a fierce argument. Finally he gave up talking and just sat and listened to her rave. Suddenly she raised her voice.

"And in addition," she shouted, "stop sitting there with your hands in your pockets making fists at me!"

---

692 "How's the wife?" an old friend asked George when they met at the service station.

"I don't know," George replied. "She isn't speaking to me and I'm in no mood to interrupt."

RAIN

693 A tourist visiting Arizona was chatting with a suntanned cowboy. "Doesn't rain ever fall here?" the out-East slicker asked.

The cowboy recollected a moment, then said,

"Remember the story of Noah and the ark and how it rained 40 days and nights?"

The tourist nodded.

"Well, we got a whole inch that time."

694 A Russian named Rudolph glanced out the window of his apartment on Christmas morning and remarked, "It's raining."

"No, listen to the patter on the roof. "It's sleeting," said the wife.

"It's raining," insisted the Russian. "Rudolph the Red knows rain, dear."

695 Rain was pouring in torrents when Mark Twain stepped out of church with a friend. "Do you think it will stop?" the friend asked the famous humorist.

"Aways has," Twain replied with a confident grin.

REALTORS

696 A realtor took a newcomer from Georgia to a new house in Chicago. "This house has absolutely no flaws," said the real estate woman.

"No flaws?" queried the southerner. "Then what do you all walk on?"

697 A realtor was showing a prospect some lowland property. "Doesn't this creek sometimes overflow the property?" the prospect asked.

"Well, yes," replied the realtor, "but look at

it another way. It's not one of those sickly creeks that's always confined to its bed."

RELATIVES

698 Two ten-year-olds were talking about the brilliance of their relatives. "My uncle is in medical school," said one.

"Is he studying medicine to be a doctor?" asked the other.

"Naw, they're studying him."

699 "Today is Cousin Mary's birth date," the wife told her husband. "We ought to give her a gift. Remember she gave me that hat with the fruit on top. We really should reciprocate."

"Reciprocate," snorted the husband. "We should retaliate."

REPORT CARDS

700 A father was scowling over his son's report card. "Only one good thing about this report. With these grades you couldn't possibly be cheating."

RESTAURANTS

701 A traveling salesman saw a sign along a Tennessee highway that said, "Jenny's Home Cooking." He stopped and tried a meal. He liked it and kept coming back each time he traveled that road, but never met anyone named Jenny. At last his curiosity pushed him to say to the manager, "I've been coming here every month for a year, but I've never seen Jenny. Where is she?"

"Like the sign says," the manager drawled. "Jenny's home cooking."

RETIREMENT

702 The big boss beamed as he handed out a retirement check to a long-time faithful employee. "Congratulations, Harvey," he said. "You have now reached the green pastures. Don't they look beautiful up ahead?"

"Sure do," said the man retiring, "but I've worked so hard for this company that I don't have the strength to climb the fences."

RIDDLES

703 What is the difference between Prince Charles, an orphan, a bald-headed man and a gorilla?

Prince Charles is an heir apparent, an orphan has ne'er a parent, a bald-headed man has no hair apparent and a gorilla has a hairy parent.

704 Rachel: What kind of seal makes music?
Andy: I don't know.
Rachel: A harp seal!

ROCKETS

705 Comrade at party headquarters calling comrade at Chinese rocket center: "Why did our first moon rocket miss by 222,334 kilometers?"

Rocket scientist: "53,456 Chinese jump on seesaw bouncer one-eighth of second too soon."

RUDENESS

706 A butcher was busy serving a customer when a large woman charged in and said, "Give me two pounds of cat food, and hurry!" Then noticing the other customer, she said, "I hope you'll excuse me for butting in. I'm really in a hurry."

The other customer forced a smile. "Of course. I always move aside for someone that's hungry."

---

707 A diner growled at the waitress as he bit into a biscuit. "You must serve dog biscuits here."

"Certainly, sir. Would you like some more now, or have them sent to your kennel?"

SALARIES

708 They call it "take-home pay" because where else can you afford to take it?

SALES PEOPLE AND SELLING

709 "Let me show you the most efficient vacuum cleaner ever made," the pushy salesman said as he dumped a sack of dirt on the housewife's clean carpet. "If this machine doesn't pick all that up, I'll eat it."

"Use this spoon," the angry housewife said. "We didn't pay our electric bill last month."

---

710 Back when binding glue was used on

books, most volumes were not sold in bookstores, but by door-to-door salesmen who frequently had to explain the odor. One book seller, anxious to make a sale, explained to his customer, "Madam, if you smell something, it's me, not the book."

711 A small time salesman sneaked aboard the millionaire's club car that took passengers to Wall Street. He listened politely to the traders around him talk about their deals. After awhile, one of the moguls turned to the newcomer and asked, "How's business with you?"

"Looking up," the little salesman replied. "Yellows were up a half million yesterday. Blues were up 300,000."

Eyes raised, the mogul queried. "What is your business?"

"Oh, I sell jelly beans," the little man replied.

712 "What's this big item on your expense account?" the sales manager asked one of his traveling salesmen.

"Oh, that," exclaimed the salesman. "That's only my motel bill.,"

"Well, just don't buy any more motels," snorted the testy boss.

713 A new real estate salesman asked his sales manager how to calm the feelings of an angry client who had just discovered his newly purchased lot was in a swamp under water. "Don't think negatively," the sales manager said. "Whatever you do, don't revoke the sale. Go back and sell him a boat and motor."

714 Shoeshine man: "Shine, Mister?"

Grumpy businessman hurrying to catch a plane: "No thanks."

Shoeshine man: "Shine 'em so you can see your face?"

Businessman: "I said, No!"

Shoeshine man: "Don't blame you."

715 Salesman to little boy at door: "Is your mother engaged at the moment?"

Little boy: "No sir, I think she's married."

716 Shoestore manager to customer: "You'd like some loafers and heels? We have a good selection. I'll send a pair to wait on you."

717 A sales manager received a sales letter from a new salesman he had hired only a few days before.

"Dear Boss: I seed this outfit whut ain't never took a penny's worth of nuthin from us before. I sole them a hunnerd thousand dollars of guds. I am now going to Oklahomeee."

Three days later, a second letter reached the home office.

"Dear Boss: I cum here to Tulsee town and I

sell these ole fellers half a milyon."

The sales manager posted both letters on the department bulletin board with a note added by the company president:

"We've been spendin' to mush time tryin' ta spel, instead of tryin' ta sel. Let's take a few tips from Gooch who is on the rode doin' a grate job fer us, and you fellers go out thar ond do lack he done."

---

718 A salesman looked at the sign on the door and gulped. It said: COME ON IN. THE GUN IS LOADED. WE SHOOT EVERY THIRD SALESMAN. THE SECOND ONE JUST LEFT.

---

719 A couple was testing furniture. The woman was rather large and got wedged in a chair. "I'm stuck on this one," she told the salesman.

"Great," he replied, "glad you like it."

SCHOOL

720 The world geography teacher asked her class, "What is the name of the principal river in Egypt?"

Smart Susie replied, "The Nile."

"Correct, now I wonder if Artie can name the Nile's smaller tributaries?"

"Sure," said Artie. "Juveniles."

---

721 Final exams were over and Junior burst

into the room where his father was sitting. "Well, Dad," he exclaimed, "we're both in the same boat. Neither of us got promoted this year."

---

722 Teacher: "Give me a sentence with an object."
    Student: "You're very pretty, teacher."
    Teacher: "What's the object?"
    Student: "A good grade."

---

723 "Children," the third grade teacher said, "give me some sentences that use the word, 'beans'."
    "My father grows beans," said one. "My mother cooks beans," said another. "I like beans," said still another.
    "We are all human beans!" said a fourth.

---

724 The guidance counselor at the junior high school was trying to inspire a shiftless boy to study harder. "Look, Jerry," he said, "if you study harder, you might become a famous inventor like Benjamin Franklin. He discovered electricity, you know."
    "Yah," Jerry said, "but I'd rather be the meter reader. He's the guy who makes all the money from electricity."

---

725 "Now, class," said the teacher, "here is a sentence that I want you to paraphrase. It is,

'He was bent on seeing her.' "

A few seconds passed, then a boy wrote, "The sight of her doubled him up."

---

726 "It's not the school I don't like," the boy told his mother. "It's the principal of the thing."

---

727 An Oklahoma school superintendent entered the hospital for a serious operation. When he came out from under the anesthetic a telegram was waiting for him. It read:

"The school board voted four to three last night to wish you a speedy recovery."

SCIENTISTS

728 A science professor was trying to impress his freshman class about the great scholars who had taught at the university. "In this very room," he said, "Dr. Reginald Huggle invented a revolutionary new explosive."

"Sir, did that spot on the wall come from his experiments?" asked a starry-eyed student.

"In a way, yes," the professor replied. "That spot is Dr. Huggle."

---

729 The wife of Robert A. Millikan, a famous physicist, happened to overhear her maid answer the telephone. "Yes," the maid said, "this is Dr. Millikan's residence, but he's not the kind of doctor who does anybody any good."

730 Luther Burbank, the famous plant scientist, was world renowned for his work with hybrids. An acquaintance, who lacked confidence in Burbank's skill, once asked him, "What are you working on now?"

Burbank replied, "I'm trying to cross an eggplant with a milkweed."

"And what do you expect to come from that?"

"Why, custard pie," said Burbank matter-of-factly.

SCOTCHMEN

731 A Scotchman had worn the same hat for 20 years and decided it was time for a new topper. With aching heart he walked into the only hat shop in his town. "Here I am again," he announced to the clerk.

732 Two Scotchmen were talking about the son of one. "I understand your son has decided to study dentistry instead of becoming an ear specialist," Mac said. "What made him change his mind?"

"Can't figure it out," replied Mike. "All I ever told him was, 'People have 32 teeth and only two ears.'"

733 Two Scotchmen were in a bank when a bandit walked in waving a gun and demanding everyone's money. One Scotchman, a quick thinker, grabbed a roll of bills and handed them to his friend. "Here's that money I borrowed from you last year."

---

734 Scotchman's letter to editor: "If you don't quit printing stories about stingy Scotchmen, I'm going to quit borrowing your paper from my neighbor."

---

735 Two Scotchman went into business and agreed that whoever died first was to have $50,000 put in his casket by the other. McMilligan died and McJenkins put in a check.

SECRETARIES

736 A secretary was habitually 20 minutes late for work each day. One morning she reached her desk only ten minutes late. "Well, Veronica," said her boss with a grim smile, "let me congratulate you. This is the earliest you've ever been late."

---

737 Irma, a secretary, was called into her boss' office. "Look at this letter," she said. "Five errors in one paragraph. What do you have to say about that?"

Irma glanced at her watch and replied indignantly. "Mr. Brewster, it's three minutes past five! You're annoying me on my own time."

~~~~~~

738 The executive was disgusted with his new secretary because she ignored the phone when it rang. Finally he reminded her, "It's one of your duties to answer the phone."

"It is?" she replied in amazement. "But it seems so foolish. All of the calls are for you."

SEEING

739 A workman had climbed a steep ladder and was perched precariously on the rim of the city hall clock. He was obviously cleaning the huge dial when a passerby stopped to watch and ask a question.

"What's the problem?" the passerby asked. "Is something wrong with the clock?"

"It's fine," replied the workman. "I'm just a little nearsighted."

SELFISHNESS

740 The smallest package in the world is a man wrapped up in himself.

SENIOR CITIZENS

741 They fixed grandma's broken rocking chair because they didn't want her to rock and roll.

~~~~~~

742 Grandpa came to the city and attended a ballerina performance with his grandchildren. After awhile, his granddaughter asked, "What do you think of this, grandpa?"

"Looks kinda stupid to me. Them girls jumpin' around on tiptoe. They should get some taller girls."

SHIPS

743 The captain of a fancy cruise ship excited the admiration of his crew and passengers by his skill in piloting the huge cruise ship. Throughout his 25 years as a skipper, his subordinates remained puzzled at a ritual he performed daily. Every morning before going to the bridge he would unlock a special compartment in his office, remove a strongbox, unlock it, remove a fading slip of paper, read it, nod, then return it to the strongbox, lock the box, replace the box in the compartment and lock the compartment.

When he finally retired, the first, second and third mates rushed to the control room to obtain the mysterious slip of paper. Breathlessly they read one sentence: "Starboard is right. Port is left."

744 A seasick passenger was taking his first trip on a luxury cruise ship. "How far are we from land, steward?" he gasped.

"Three miles, sir."

"Oh, good. Which way?"

"Straight down, sir."

SHOOTING

745 There was a cowboy who could shoot so fast the gun didn't even leave his holster. They called him, "No-toes Hickok."

SIGHTSEEING

746 A ratchety tour guide in an Ozark town that had become famous for celebrity country music theaters told his group, "We'll begin our tour at Joe's Flea Market. That way, you can start from scratch."

SIGNS

747 Sign in auto repair shop: "We guarantee our work and stand in front of every brake job."

748 Sign at the entrance to a small community: "Drive carefully. Our children may be disobeying us."

749 Sign in front of a service station: "Put a Tiger in Your Tank."

Further down the highway, another station advertised: "Our Final Filters Remove Tiger Hairs."

750 Sign on a repair shop for foreign cars: "Old Volks' Home."

751 Sign announcing a highway crew ahead: "Slow Men Working."

752 Sign used by a drive-in psychiatrist: "Toot and Tell."

753 Sign in police station: "Every Drunk Driver Needs a Cop for a Chaser."

754 Sign at the beginning of a long crooked stretch of highway: "Sleepy Drivers Rest in Pieces."

755 Slogan for auto safety: "Help Save Lives — Go On a Crash Diet."

756 A country lady became aggravated by cars driving by fast on the dusty road and soiling her wash. So she posted this sign on both sides of the house: DRIVE SLOW. BIG WASHOUT AHEAD.

757 Notice in a small service station and grocery at the edge of a Western desert: "Please don't ask for information. If we knew anything, we wouldn't be here."

758 Statement on a church bulletin board: "If absence makes the heart grow fonder, lots of folks must love our church."

759 Sign on cabinetmaker's truck: "You Should See What I Saw."

760 Sign above door of finance company office which customers see upon leaving: "Be Careful Driving Home. The Life You Save May Be our Loan."

761 Sign in dentist's office: "Weak Batteries Cause Cavities. Have You Checked Your Electric Toothbrush Lately?"

762 Sign on a store: "Closed — Opened by Mistake."

763 Sign on a rundown service station: "Open When We're Here. Closed When We're Not."

764 Sign on an out-of-business store: "We Undersold Everybody."

SIN

765 "What are sins of omission?" a Sunday school teacher asked his pupils.

"Those are sins you ought to have committed, but haven't got around to yet," answered a boy.

∞∞∞∞∞∞∞∞∞∞∞∞∞∞∞∞∞∞∞∞∞∞∞∞∞∞∞∞

766 President Calvin Coolidge was known for giving short answers. One Sunday his wife was unable to accompany him to church. When he returned, Mrs. Coolidge asked, "What did the pastor talk about, Calvin?"

"Sin," he said tersely.

"What did he say about sin?"

"He was against it."

SKEPTICS

767 A skeptical fellow and his wife were traveling through a Western state. As they watched the scenery through the train window, the wife remarked, "See those sheep on the mesa. They've just been sheared."

The skeptic peered through his glasses. "So they seem to have been — on this side."

SKY DIVERS

768 A group of giggling high school girls were interviewing a handsome veteran sky diver for their school paper. "You must have had some exciting experiences, even some dangerous ones, "the editor cooed.

"I certainly have," said the sky diver. "Why, once I jumped from 20,000 feet and came through some stormy clouds, and...."

"Yes, yes," the girls murmured in chorus, "and then what?"

"I floated safely through the clouds into the clear air and then I saw the sign that said KEEP OFF THE GRASS!"

SLEEP

769 Why did the night watchman keep falling asleep atop the Empire State Building? Investigating doctors found it was because the skyscraper was built on bed rock.

770 Uncle Elmer arrived late for a Christmas visit with his relatives. He had to sleep on a lumpy couch in the living room. Next morning, his sister asked if he slept well.

"Pretty good," he drawled. "From time to time I got up and rested."

771 Mister Ed, television's famous talking horse, defined midnight as the hour "when it's too early to hit the hay — and too late to eat it."

772 "We go to bed with the chickens," the farmer told his city visitor.

"In town, we'd rather sleep in our own beds," replied the city slicker.

SMALL TOWNS

773 Uncle Ben described his country town as "not having much get up and go." Because, he said, "when you get up there ain't no place to go."

~~~~~~

774 A Missouri college student described his home town in which he was reared as a poke-and-plumb town. "Drive through," he said, "and by the time you poke your thumb out the window, you're plumb out of town."

SMOKING

775 Smokers do a double-take when they see this sign at a service station: "No smoking. If your life isn't worth anything, our gasoline is."

~~~~~~

776 A fellow can't win. A man gave up smoking and began chewing toothpicks. He died six months later of Dutch Elm disease.

SNOW

777 When snow began falling, a man in Minnesota went outside and filled a small box with the white stuff. "What are you doing that for?" his wife called from the doorway.

"I'm going to mail it to my brother, Gus, down in Florida. Might make him homesick."

"But it will be gone before it gets there," his wife said.

"Of course not," replied the husband. "Who would be mean enough to steal a little snow?"

SOCIALISM

778 A man in a socialist country was being examined for loyalty to the state. "If you had a million dollars, would you give half to the state?"

"Sure," he said.

"If you had 5,000 acres of rich farm land, would you give three fourths to the state?"

"Certainly."

"If you had two pair of trousers, would you give one to the state?"

"No."

"Why not?"

"Because, I've got two pair of trousers."

---

779 Reporters from a free enterprise country were touring a huge factory in a socialist nation. Their guide would talk about almost everything except what the factory made. Finally, one of the newsmen slipped aside to speak to a worker. "What do you make here?" he whispered.

"Oh, just signs that say, 'This machine is out of order.'"

---

780 A long line of people were lined up in front of a socialized medicine clinic in London. There was a good deal of shoving and pushing, and the irritation of those in the line was increased by a little man who kept trying to get to the head of the line. After he was forcibly pushed back to the end for the fourth time, he yelled, "Okay you nincompoops, if I get shoved back once more, I won't open the clinic today."

SONS

781 Two boys were arguing about the accomplishments of their fathers. "You know Lake Michigan?" said one. "Well, my dad's a construction worker and he dug the hole for it."

"Ah, that's nothing," snorted the other. "Have you ever heard of the Dead Sea? My dad's an exterminator. He killed it."

SOUTHERNERS

782 A southern grandfather was bragging about his smart granddaughter who had just graduated from a large southern university. "Yep," he crowed, "Betty Jane graduated magnolia cum louder and was voted 'most likely to secede.'"

SPACE TRAVEL (ALSO SEE ROCKETS)

783 Before astronaut Gordon Cooper was strapped into a space capsule, he told a reporter he was worried. "Why should you be?" asked the reporter. "Think of what you're doing for your country."

"I know," said Cooper. "But I've got to remember every gadget and dial in this machine. I'm thinking that each one was made by the lowest bidder."

784 In the year 2005 an American space explorer landed on a strange planet. Suddenly a group of strange, furry creatures appeared before him. "Take me to your leader," the American requested.

One of the furry creatures led him through a maze of tunnels, past hundreds of other furry creatures, until they reached a huge throne room. There he met the leader, who looked just like the other creatures except for a huge tube sticking out of the top of his head.

"What are you creatures?" the American asked.

"We're Furries," the guide said.

"What do you call yourself?" the American asked the leader.

"I'm the Furry with the syringe on top."

SPEAKERS AND SPEAKING

785 Speakers that should have stayed home:

The speaker that exhausted his listeners before he exhausted his subject.

The speaker who went down deeper, stayed under longer and came up drier.

786 The banquet speaker was droning on. "Some people are born great, some achieve greatness and some..." He paused to catch his breath just long enough for a tired man to mumble, "...And some just grate on you."

787 Too many speeches are like a wheel — the longer the spoke, the greater the tire.

788 Will Rogers was emceeing a banquet at which a speaker talked for too long. Said Rogers after the bore finally quit, "Ladies and Gentlemen, you have been listening to the famous Chinese statesman, Mr. On Too Long."

789 The boring speaker ran on and on and on. Finally the chairman made a motion with the gavel to stop him. But he missed and hit the man sitting next to him. As he was falling underneath the table, this man groaned, "Hit me again. I can still hear him."

790 The coffee's cold,
The speaker drones,
Please heed the rule:
Be brief, be swift, be gone!

791 Cut and dried speeches need more cutting and less drying.

792 Two politicians opposing one another for the same office were invited to speak at a county fair. When the first finished, the second rose and said, "My honorable opponent's speech was like the horns of a steer: A point here. A point there. And a lot of bull between."

793 A certain man in a community had a talent for after-dinner speaking. One evening at a ladies Sunday school class party his wife was asked which after-dinner speech of his she preferred.

"I think," said the long-suffering wife, "that the best after-dinner speech I ever heard him give — and this was just once, was this: 'Dear, I'll help with the dishes tonight.'"

~~~~~~

794 When Dr. Frank Leavell, founder of the Baptist Student Union, was to speak at a compulsory college chapel, he would begin by saying, "There are three things very difficult to do. One is to climb over a fence that is leaning towards you. Another is to kiss a girl that is leaning away from you. And another is to speak at a compulsory chapel."

After pausing for this to sink in, he would continue, "I haven't tried the first. The second is none of your business. And the third won't be too difficult if you will cooperate with me."

~~~~~~

795 A toastmaster said to the guest speaker as the coffee was being served. "Should we let them enjoy themselves a little longer, or would you rather give your talk now?"

~~~~~~

796 Advice from Texas to banquet speakers: If you don't strike oil in five minutes, stop boring.

~~~~~~

797 Lament of a banquet speaker's wife:
If he can recall so many jokes
With all the things that mold them,

Why can't he recall with equal skill,
How many times he told them?

---

798 The powerful speaker stepped confidently to the podium and said: "I'm like the furnace that got fired by the janitor — all ready to blast off."

---

799 "Do you always keep a rope tied around your waist?" the old lady asked the explorer at a lecture.

"Yes, madam," he replied. "It has saved my life many times."

"How awful," the woman gushed. "Don't you feel terribly nervous hanging from a rope?"

"Not exactly nervous," he said, "just high strung."

---

800 A minister returned to give his first chapel address at New Orleans Baptist Theological Seminary, the school from which he had graduated. Before him swam a sea of student faces. Behind him sat the austere faculty and in the deep chair near the pulpit sat the president, Dr. Roland Q. Leavell. The speaker began by mentioning his apprehensions and said, "This is going to be hard for me. I'm between the devil and the deep blue sea."

At that remark, President Leavell arose and said, "This is the first time I've ever been compared to the deep blue sea."

801 A man was seated beside his wife at the speaker's table. While he was being introduced, the man's wife slipped him a note on which was printed in large letters, KISS. The speaker was thinking how nice this was when he read the smaller letters that made the note complete. "Keep it short, stupid."

802 A famed entomologist came to talk to a group of ninth graders about the danger of rat infestation. The young people listened attentively, then when the lecture was over, one girl rose to speak the class' thanks. She ended by saying, "We didn't even know what a rat looked like until you came to our school."

803 "You, sir," said the politician to his opponent, "speak to the selfish whims of this generation. I speak for posterity."

"I agree," replied the second office seeker, "and you seem determined to speak until the arrival of your audience."

804 Abraham Lincoln said that probably only one-sixth of the stories attributed to him were his own. He added, "I don't claim to have invented anything original; I'm just a retail dealer."

805 Said the boring speaker, "And what more can I talk about?"

Replied a tired voice from the audience, "Ten seconds."

806 Mark Twain grew tired of being called upon to make impromptu speeches whenever he was invited out to dinner. He finally made it a requisite of his acceptance that he would not be asked to speak.

Later, at a gathering, he rose from his chair near the end of dinner. Suddenly all talk stopped and the crowd exploded with loud applause. When the applause quieted, Twain cleared his throat and called, "Waiter, please bring me some bread."

807 Mark Twain was so scared when time came for his first speech that his hosts promised to place people at various places in the audience who would laugh at appropriate times. Twain then brought the house down with his opening: "Julius Caesar is dead, Shakespeare is dead, Napoleon is dead, Abraham Lincoln is dead and I'm not feeling so well myself."

808 Georgia glossary: ABODE — Plank. MARNIN' — A.M. TARRED — Weary. WRETCHED — proper name for Dick. HARMONY — A favorite food. CALLER —

That part of the shirt which goes around the neck. BONE — Coming of a new baby into the world. RAH CHAIR — Where you are. BECKON — served with eggs and biscuits.

~~~~~~

809 Mark Twain, in making an after-dinner speech, said:

"Speaking of eggs, I'm reminded of the town of Squash where I went to lecture. I thought I'd find out if the people knew anything at all about what was in store for them. So I turned in at the general store.

" 'Good afternoon, friend,' I said to the storekeeper. 'Any entertainment here tonight to help a stranger while away an evening?'

"The storekeeper, who was sorting mackerel, straightened up, wiped his hands on his apron, and said: 'I expect there's goin' to be a lecture. I've been sellin' eggs all day.' "

SPELLING

810 A hillbilly asked his wife to spell rat. "R A T," she spelled.

"No, Liza," he said. "I mean like rat (right) chere (here)."

~~~~~~

811 E may be the most tragic letter in the alphabet because it's always out of "cash," always in "debt," and never out of "danger." But it's always in "peace," never in "war," in something to "eat," the start of "existence," the beginning and the ending of "ease" and the climax of "trouble."

SPINSTERS

812 A defiant spinster lady who died at 99 added this note to her will: "Please do not put 'Miss' on my tombstone. I haven't missed anything important in life."

813 "Ah, if I could only have two wishes granted," a spinster lady said to her friend.

"What would they be?" the friend asked.

"I'd use the first wish for a husband."

"And the second?"

"I'd save it until I found out how he treated me."

814 When America's space program was booming, a spinster lady looked up from the newspaper one afternoon and said to her woman friend, "My, all this money to land a man on the moon. I'd be happy just to land one on the earth."

TIPPING

815 It is the custom in England for a theater goer to tip the usher who seats him. On this occasion, a murder mystery was about to begin, staged so the audience would not know the murderer until the last line of the play.

A Scotchman, who was led to his seat, slipped the usher a small coin. The usher felt it in the darkness and whispered back to the tight tipper, "Don't tell anyone, old chap, but it was the maid who killed the master of the house."

~~~~~~

816 A well-dressed woman smilingly permitted the bellboy to roll her six suitcases to her room on the 65th floor of a swank hotel. Then she tipped him a dime. He looked at the coin and bowed solemnly, "Madam, how would you like your change?"

TOURISTS

817 Tourist to native: "What are those things floating in the bay?"

Native: "Buoys."

Tourist: "And what are those crazy birds circling overhead?"

Native: "Gulls."

Tourist: "That figures. The gulls always go where the buoys are."

TOWNS

818 A tourist traveling to Calico Rock, Arkansas got on a back road. He thought he was going toward the town when he saw a highway sign pointing in the opposite direction. He turned around, drove back a few miles and found a native.

"Am I headed for Calico Rock?" he asked.

"Nope, it's back the way you come."

"But I saw a sign pointing this way."

"Yep, but they made that sign for the other side, only there was a rock ledge there, so they put it on this side."

"Well, that's a big help to a driver, especially

a stranger!"

"Can't hep that," said the native. "Ever'body should know where Calico Rock is."

~~~~~~

819 A Russian highway engineer was telling an American counterpart of how Communist officials in the old Soviet Union renamed towns. Illville was changed to Dawn, Horse to Red Berry, Foul Hole to New Orchard, Toad Village to Azure, Swineroo to Sunrise and Plunderville to Park City."

"We've got some towns that could stand renaming," the American said. "Henpeck, Illinois and Nogo, Arkansas for starters."

TRACK

820 An American track coach asked a Communist Chinese track coach how he had trained his runners to break three world records. "That's easy," said the Chinese. "We use real bullets in our starting guns."

TRADING

821 Abraham Lincoln and a judge friend were talking about horse trading, when Lincoln proposed: "Judge, I'll trade horses with you under these conditions: Neither of us will see the other's horse until we see it produced here in the courtyard of this hotel. If either of us backs out of the agreement, he forfeits $25 to the other."

The judge agreed and both left to obtain a horse for trade while a crowd gathered to watch the fun. After awhile the judge appeared leading a bony nag that was blind in both eyes. Lincoln came bearing a carpenter's saw-horse on his shoulder.

Lincoln set the saw-horse on the ground and carefully examined the judge's horse. "Well, Judge," he said in mock disgust, "this is the first time I ever got the worst of it in a horse trade."

TRAFFIC AND TRAVELING

822 Riddle:

Always runs, never walks;
Has a tongue, but never talks.
Answer: A farm wagon.

823 A backwoodsman came to the big city to see the sights and registered for a room at a hotel. Before he left, the clerk said, "Breakfast is from 6:30 to 9:30, lunch from 12 to 3:30 and dinner from 5 to 9.

"But if that's true," said the new guest, "when will I get to see the sights?"

824 A suburbanite caught in a traffic jam on the way home saw his neighbor walking along the sidewalk. "Need a lift?" he asked.

"No thanks," said the neighbor. "I'm in a hurry."

825 A driver ran a stop light and was halted by an officer down the block. "Didn't you see that red light?" the policeman asked.

"Certainly," the driver said, "I've got contacts."

"I don't care if you have," the policeman went on. "I'm giving you a ticket anyway."

826 "Wait," the policeman said. "You can't park here."

"Why not?" asked the motorist. "Doesn't that sign say, 'Fine for Parking'?"

827 Brown to his brother: "Says here a man gets run over every half hour in New York City."

Brother: "Wow! He really must be a mess!"

828 Mark Twain told about a traveler on the frontier who found himself, when night came on, in a wild region. A tremendous thunderstorm brought torrential rain. His horse gave out and he had to follow the muddy trail alone. Occasional flashes of lightning kept him from becoming lost, while thunder shook the earth under him.

Finally one bolt brought him to his knees. Not a regular praying man, his petition was brief and to the point: "Oh, Lord! If it's all the same to you, give us a little more light and a little less noise."

TRAINS

829 Sign at railroad crossing: "A train crosses this intersection at nine a.m. and six p.m.

whether your car is on it or not."

---

830 A businessman got on an Amtrak train at New York City's Grand Central Station in the afternoon and called a porter aside. "I'm dead tired and am going to my compartment to sleep. Be sure and wake me at eight in the morning when we go through Pittsburgh, Pennsylvania. Don't miss doing this, for I have an appointment there to put through one of the biggest business deals of my life."

The businessman fell asleep and when he finally awoke the train was pulling into Cleveland, Ohio. He called for the porter and gave him a tongue lashing, saying that he planned to report the incident to every Amtrak official in the country.

After the angry businessman had gotten off that train to catch another back to Pittsburgh, another porter came up to the victim of the tongue lashing and said, "I've never heard such language."

"I have and worse," the first porter said. "You should have heard what the fellow said that I put off in Pittsburgh."

---

831 A crack Amtrak train shrieked to a sudden halt. A woman passenger picked herself up off the floor and looked hard at the conductor who was helping up passengers. "What happened?" she asked.

"We hit a horse," he said.

"Was it on the tracks?"

"No, lady, the engineer had to chase it across a field."

TRUCKERS

832 Three slightly deaf truckers rolled up to a stop. "Windy, ain't it?" said one.

"No it isn't," disagreed another. "It's Thursday."

"Me, too," said the third. "Let's have a cup of coffee."

833 Barney, a long distance truck driver, was telling his experiences to some of the boys back at Chimney Corners. "Boys, I took a load of stuff to New York City and saw the biggest elevator I ever saw. It was so big that I could drive my rig right in it. I delivered the goods on the top of the building, then drove off the edge."

"How did you survive?" they asked.

"Warn't no problem. My air brakes stopped me halfway to the ground."

TROUBLE

834 How you can know when it'going to be a bad day:

You call Suicide Prevention and they put you on hold.

Mike Wallace calls from "60 Minutes" saying they are investigating your business.

Your birthday cake collapses from the weight of the candles.

Your twin sister forgot your birthday.

You turn on the news and they're showing

emergency routes out of the city.

Your boss tells you not to bother taking off your coat.

The bird singing outside your window is a buzzard.

You wake up and can't open your mouth — your braces are locked together.

Your income tax check bounces.

You put both contact lenses in the same eye.

Your pet rock snaps at you.

UMPIRES

835 Suffering from headaches, a baseball umpire went to an optician. After a thorough checkup, the doctor said, "You need glasses."

The ump leaped to his feet and jerked his thumb. "That'll cost you $100," he growled, "and you're out of the game for today."

---

836 When Dizzy Dean was a pitcher, he once spent a hot afternoon arguing with a plate umpire's calls on balls and strikes. The celebrated pitcher, who later became a game broadcaster, never once persuaded the umpire to change his mind and the other team won the game two to one.

That evening Dizzy ran into the official at a restaurant. "We had quite a game today," he said. "Too bad you didn't get to see it."

UNIONS

837 "What are you doing?" the foreman asked the bricklayer.

"Sharpening a pencil."

"Okay, but look out that the union doesn't see you. That's a carpenter's job."

VACATIONS

838 Marriage counselor to quarreling husband and wife: "You two need a vacation."

Wife, holding up hand: "No, sir. We can't agree on that. My idea of a vacation is getting away from it all. His idea is to take it all with us."

839 "Made your vacation plans yet?" the junior executive asked his counterpart in another department.

"No, the wife and I can't agree on where to go. I'd like to take a trip around the world, but Mary wants to go another place."

VACATION BIBLE SCHOOL

840 A little boy had just returned from his first session in a church Vacation Bible School. "Mother, what's a witches' stand?" he asked.

His mother looked perplexed. "Whatever did they teach you in that church?"

"Oh, they marched us in, and then we faced the American flag and recited '...to the republic for witches' stand.'"

VENTRILOQUISTS

841 The detective looked tired and worried as he burst into the chief's office. "Look, Chief," he said, "We've given that ventriloquist the third degree, and so far two stenographers, three patrolmen and I have confessed to the crime. Should we continue?"

VETERINARIANS

842 A veterinarian also served as the part-time police chief in the small town. One night the phone rang and the caller asked the vet's wife, "Is the doc there?"

"He's here," said the wife, "but do you want him as a police chief or as a veterinarian?"

After a short pause, the caller said, "A little bit of both, I reckon. We can't get our St. Bernard to open his mouth, and there's a prowler in it."

WAGES

843 A country boy did a hauling job for a retired couple from the city. He submitted his bill of $4.50 for the following labor: "Three goes and three comebacks at six bits per went."

WAITERS AND WAITRESSES

844 Customer: "Waiter, I demand to see the manager. I've never experienced anything as tough as this steak in my life."

Waiter: "You will, sir, if I call the manager!"

---

845 "How's our spring chicken, sir?" the waiter asked.

"That's the right description," the patron replied. "I just broke a tooth on one of the springs."

846 A customer yelled to the waiter, "This soup isn't fit for a hog!"

"Sorry, sir," said the waiter. "I'll take it back and bring you some that is."

847 "Hey, waitress, I asked for some strawberry shortcake and you only brought me a plate of strawberries. What happened to the cake?"

"Oh, dear, did I? That must be what we're short of."

WATCHMEN

848 A night watchman heard strange noises in the plant. He shouted, "Come out with your hands in the air, so I can see who you is, or I'm comin' in to see who you was."

WATER

849 Wyoming has a geyser called "Old Faithful," but there's a water fountain in a Florida restaurant termed, "Old Faceful."

850 A newcomer to the city was applying for a job at the water company. "Say," he asked the personnel clerk, "is waterworks all one word, or do you spell it with a hydrant?"

WEALTH

851 Mark Twain was talking to a man who was envious of the wealth of the steel magnate, Andrew Carnegie. "After all," said the man in a superior tone, "like all of these great fortunes, Carnegie's money is tainted."

"Yes," agreed Twain, " 'tain't yours, and 'tain't mine."

WEATHER

852 A man from the Miami, Florida Chamber of Commerce was speaking to a convention of travel agents in a hotel ballroom. The promoter was listing all the things visitors could do in Miami, when a man burst in with a warning that a winter storm was sweeping in from the north with possible snow flurries and below freezing temperatures in the northern suburbs. Heavy snow was already reported in Atlanta where many Miami-bound airline flights had been canceled. The man urged the travel agents to check their flight connections and make plans accordingly.

The promoter's face paled in embarrassment. Finally, he said, "Georgia and South Carolina are sending in some terrible weather, aren't they?"

WEDDINGS

853 Bridesmaid: "What will you be thinking of when you walk up the aisle as the wedding march plays?"

Bride: "Boy, aisle altar him."

854 "Don't go throwing rice on my bald head," said the usher at the wedding reception. "It might sprout and squash you."

855 Two fellows were teeing off on the first fairway when a beautiful girl in a bride's dress came running across the grass screaming at one, "Bill, how could you leave me waiting at the church?"

The golfer named Bill patiently looked up from where he had been measuring his swing and said firmly, "Didn't I tell you — only if it rains!"

856 A minister got confused at the close of the wedding ceremony and said to the audience, "You may now view the remains."

857 A man stood quietly away from the rice-throwing crowd as the newly married couple ran down the aisle of the church. Finally the man was approached by a guest at the wedding. "You look sad. Is the bride a favorite niece?"

The man slowly shook his head. "No relation. I'm just the janitor. With all that rice and confetti, I'm thinking of tomorrow."

858 The minister said to the middle-aged

maiden lady who was being married, "Do you take this man for better or for worse?"

She replied, "I'm taking him as he is."

---

859 The slothful tailor failed to get the groom his trousers in time for the wedding. So the groom sued for promise of breeches.

---

860 Said one young thing to another at a wedding: "They met at a travel agency. She was his last resort."

---

861 A minister slipped in a wedding ceremony and said, "I now unite you in holy deadlock and pronounce you man and wife."

WELFARE

862 A little boy spent his allowance by the middle of the week and came around to his father for some advice on making some extra money. When the father said nothing, the little boy suggested, "How about putting me on welfare?"

WIVES

863 Difference between secretary and wife: "One takes dictation. The other gives it."

---

864 A businessman in Dallas received a call

from his brother in Oklahoma saying their father had died. "What were father's last words?" the brother in Dallas asked.

Replied the other brother: "He had none. Mother was with him to the end."

---

865 A woman made a deposit for a layaway item. "How long do you wish for us to hold it?" the clerk asked.

"Until my husband does something unforgivable," she replied.

---

866 A man was stopped for speeding. "Where's the fire?" the cop asked.

"I wasn't going to a fire," the man said. "You see my wife's garden club is having a thrift sale and I was hurrying home to save my other suit."

---

867 A woman bought an old lamp in a thrift store. When she got home and began to polish the lamp, a genie appeared.

"I am the genie of the lamp," he proclaimed. "I will grant you three wishes. You can wish for what ever you want, however, there is one condition. Whatever you wish for, your husband will receive double."

The woman thought for a minute and said, "Okay, I'm ready. For my first wish I wish you to make me extremely attractive."

The genie reminded her, "You realize that that means your husband will be twice as attractive."

"Yes, I know," replied the woman.

Poof, her wish was granted.

"For my second wish, I wish for ten million dollars, and yes, I know, my husband will get 20 million."

"Your wish is granted," intoned the genie. "And now, what is your third wish?"

The woman grinned and said, "I want you to scare me half to death."

868 "Will you love me when I'm old and wrinkled?" asked the insecure wife.

"Who says I don't?" mumbled the husband behind his newspaper.

869 An executive was telling his fishing buddy, "Yesterday I went home two hours before my wife got off from work. I had a delicious meal waiting when she arrived. Then I served her favorite desert, brewed her a cup of honey tea and brought her slippers. Next I built a fire in the fireplace and brought her favorite magazine. Then..."

The friend cut in. "And then you told her you wanted to take three days off and go fishing with me."

870 Some wives are like fishermen. They brag about the one that got away, and grumble about the one they caught.

WOMEN

871 Confusion is one woman plus one yellow traffic light. Excitement is two women plus a new secret. Chaos is three women plus one bargain. Hopefulness is four women plus a new low-calorie diet.

872 A woman job-seeker was filling out an application blank. She hesitated at the line that asked her age. The interviewer leaned over her shoulder and whispered, "The longer you wait, the harder it gets."

873 A woman who was worried about losing the bloom of her youth pleaded into her looking glass, "Mirror, mirror on the wall, who is the fairest of them all?"

The mirror took the Fifth Amendment.

874 New sports writer to his managing editor: "What shall I write about the two women with technicolor hair who screamed so much at the game?"

"Just say, 'The bleachers went wild.' "

875 A woman may be taken for granted but she never goes without saying.

876 Several women were confessing their

faults. One said, "My worst fault is vanity. I spend hours before the mirror admiring my beauty."

"That's not vanity," gushed another. "That's imagination."

877 A woman with poise is one who can look at caterpillars without feeling them crawling all over her.

878 "Look at her new hat," one envious woman said to her next-door neighbor as another neighbor left the house. "Isn't she flighty?"

"I should say so. Every time her husband gets a raise, she gets a new hat. Her husband's success must be going to her head."

879 A woman is like a newspaper, because:
Both are well worth looking over.
There's little demand for bold-faced type.
They always have the last word.
Both have forms.
Back numbers are not in demand.
Every man should have one of his own and not go around looking for another man's.

880 A beautiful woman fascinates a man; a brilliant one interests him; a good one inspires him; but a sympathetic one gets him.

881 Some men call a ten-mile hike training in physical fitness. Some women call it window shopping.

882 A guide once led a party of husbands and wives to a point overlooking Niagara Falls. Then he said, "We can now hear the mighty roar of the waters if the ladies will stop talking a moment."

883 Have you heard about the young woman's Sunday school class, aged 21-25, that called themselves, "Fishers of Men"?

WORDS

884 Grey Advertising of New York City listed some common words that often acquire hidden meanings. Examples:

Creative — an idea from "Cloud Nine."

Theoretical — an idea I don't agree with.

Practical — an idea I do agree with.

Technical — an idea I don't understand.

Simple — something I can understand.

Realistic — an idea that is not radical.

Complex — a word not in my active vocabulary.

WORK & WORKERS

885 Hay is what we must make between the time we get out of it and the time we hit it again.

886 An office manager for a bread company posted this sign: "Bread may be the staff of life, but that's no reason the life of this staff should be one continual loaf."

887 Al: "What's your brother doing now? Didn't you tell me he was applying for a government job?

Sal: "Nothing. He got the job."

888 A personnel manager was reviewing the job form an applicant had filled out. "You put here that you left your last job because of illness. What was wrong with you?"

"Well, it was kind of a mutual sickness," said the applicant. "I got sick of them and they got sick of me."

889 Personnel manager: "For this position we must have a highly responsible employee."

Applicant: "That's me. When anything went wrong where I worked before, the boss said I was responsible."

890 A woman wrote on a job application that she was 30 years old and had worked 25 years at her previous job. When the personnel director asked if she had been the boss's daughter, she replied, "No, I started at 18 and put in a lot of overtime."

~~~~~~

891 A young man marched up to the desk and interrupted the boss while he was in the middle of an important project. "Do you have an opening for a promising, smart, eager young fellow?" the job seeker asked.

The boss looked up with a frown. "Yes, I do, but don't slam it as you leave."

~~~~~~

892 A general contractor drove up to the site of his newest development and saw his workmen digging feverishly in a trench some distance from the street. "What's the idea?" he called. "The plans don't call for a trench over there. Say, where's the foreman?"

One of the workmen stopped shoveling and replied, "Trench caved in." Then he went back to work.

"Doesn't the foreman know what happened?" the contractor asked.

"If he doesn't," another shoveler replied, "we'll tell him as soon as we dig him out."

~~~~~~

893 A worker who had just been fired was talking to a friend. "When I told the boss I was executive timber and deserved a raise, he gave me the ax."

~~~~~~

894 A section foreman was known as a hard driver. One day he shouted to a man who was digging a small ditch, "Hey, Joe, you should lift your pick higher off the ground."

"I would," Joe said, "but you hang over my shoulder so much that I'm afraid of smacking you in the eye."

---

895 The new office boy was the slowest thing the vice president had ever seen on two feet. It took him 15 minutes to empty one waste basket and an hour to deliver a letter on the next floor. Finally, the vp screamed, "Ned, isn't there anything you can do in a hurry?"

The office boy thought for five minutes, then said, "I can get tired in a hurry."

---

896 "In case of nuclear attack," the office manager told his employees, "hide under the waste basket. It hasn't been hit yet."

---

897 "You look like a bum," a wife told her husband who sprawled on the porch.

"Oh, yeah," he replied. "Who brings home the unemployment check?"

---

898 Hearing the big explosion at the new factory, a reporter for the town paper came running. "What caused it?" he yelled to a workman covered with dust.

"It was that blankety-blank Lem," the workman said. "He was carrying three sticks of dynamite when the quitting whistle blew."

899 A ditch digger became a window washer. He stopped back to admire his first job and....

WRITERS

900 A would-be writer mailed story after story to an editor. Each work was terrible, but the editor sent each manuscript back with a courteous rejection slip. With the 15th submission, the editor's patience wore thin. He mailed back the submission with a note saying, "I'm returning this paper. Someone typed on it."

DAFFYNITIONS

A

Abominable Snowman: What the kids built in front of the garage door.

Adult: A person who has stopped growing at both ends and is growing in the middle.

Alarm Clock: An infernal machine that scares the daylights into you.

Alarm Clock: A device that wakens parents who have no babies.

Alimony: Price a woman charges for name dropping.

Amendments: Patches on Grandpa's overalls.

Ancient Times: When they called a cigarette a coffin nail and people laughed.

Apology: The last word which a man has in an argument with his wife.

Astronaut in Reverse: Fellow who thinks the world

revolves around himself.

Astronomer: A person whose business is looking up.

Auction: Place where you get something for nodding.

Avaricious: Itching when you should be scratching for money.

Average Man: The one whom everybody thinks they're above.

B

Bachelor: Man who never Mrs. a woman. A rolling stone who gathers no boss (Fred Allen). An eligible mass of obstinacy surrounded by suspicion (Bob Hope).

Baby Sitter: A person who is paid hush money.

Bank President: Bankerchief.

Barbecue: Family smokeout.

Barbershop: A joint where you pay money to get clipped.

Barbershop Quartet: Four popular singers who never got waited on.

Beastly Weather: When it's raining cats and dogs.

Beauty Parlor: Place where the talk is warm enough to curl a woman's hair.

Best man: The fellow your wife dated before she married you.

Bigamist: Heavy fog over New York Harbor.

DAFFYNITIONS

Big Bore: A fast gun of small caliber.

Bikini: A teeny garment that enables women to go naked in clothes.

Bill Collector: Someone who doesn't believe in putting off till tomorrow what can be dunned today.

Bird-brain: Ornithologist.

Birthday Cake: When lit with candles, it makes light of your age.

Blind Date: Someone you hope will be a vision, but turns out to be a sight.

B.O.: A smell on a swell.

Boss: The guy who rises early to see who came in late.

Branding Iron: A hot tip.

Bridal Path: Where the "groom" acquires a "Halter."

Bucking Bronco: A horse that ate a dollar bill.

Budget: An effort to live below your yearnings.

Bus Driver: A man who gets away with telling people where to get off.

C

Cabinetmaker: The president.

Capital Crime: Spending our money in Washington.

Careless Skier: One who breaks skis instead of legs.

Caterpillar: A worm wearing a fur coat.

Clodhopper: A rabbit farmer.

Claustrophobia: An Alaskan in Texas.

Commencement Gown: Grad rags.

Committee: The unable appointed by the unwilling to do the unnecessary for the ungrateful.

Committee Work: Like a reclining chair. Easy to get into, but hard to get out of.

Compulsive Credit Buyer: A man who believes that living within his income is a fate worse than debt.

Conceited Sailor: He joined the Navy so the world could see him.

Conference: Meeting of the bored.

Consultant: Person who looks at at the company flow chart and tells you if you'll have a job next year.

Copperhead: Police chief or superintendent.

Corral: Where you can get a lot of horse scents.

Crickets: Cheap enough to chirp.

Crocodile(Dial): Jar filled with soap.

Cynic: One who smells a flower and looks around for the coffin. (H.L. Mencken)

D

Dead Author: One who writes a book in a cemetery so it will have a plot.

Diet Call for a Texan: Remember the alamode (Alamo).

Dieter: Someone who eats less and less while talking about it more and more.

DAFFYNITIONS

Discouraged Dentist: He got bored with his practice because he was always down in the mouth.

Disneyland: People trap built by a mouse.

Dress Designing: What a her does to a hem to help another her get a him.

Drive-in Bank: Where cars can see their real owners.

Dual Household: House with two cars, two TV sets, two bathrooms and two opinions on every subject.

Dumb Son: Chip off the old chump.

E

Early Riser: Those who get up in time to see a late, late, late movie on TV.

Economy Flight: Where instead of showing movies, the pilot shows slides of his family vacation.

Editor: One who separates the wheat from the chaff and prints the chaff.

Electrician: Man who doesn't shock you until you get his bill.

Engagement Ring: A glittering tourniquet worn on the left hand to stop circulation.

Expert: One who can hit the bullseye without shooting the bull.

F

Fad: In one era and out the other.

Family Man: A father who has replaced the currency in his wallet with snapshots.

Farewell: As the dog said to the bone, "It's been nice gnawing you."

Farmer: A man outstanding in his field.

Filing Cabinet: Where you lose things in an orderly manner.

Fink: The result of crossing a fox with a mink.

Flattery: Telling someone what he really thinks of himself.

Flueologist: Chimney sweep.

Freeway traffic jam: Blocked artery.

Frustrated Woman: One with a live secret without access to a telephone.

G

Gazelle: A passenger reading a newspaper over another person's shoulder on a city bus.

Gentleman Horse: One, who when he comes to a fence, lets the rider go over first.

Go-getter: Husband whose wife works. All he must do is go-get-her.

Good Old Days: When men rode chargers instead of marrying them.

Gossip: Someone who puts two and two together and gets "Whew!"

H

Haul of Learning: TV quiz show.

Hypocrite: Someone who prays to God on Sunday and preys on people the rest of the week.

Hollywood Necklace: Worn by movie stars and made from old wedding rings.

Hot Line: One telephone line in a house with four teenagers.

Housewife: Pan-handler.

Husband With Decided Opinions: His wife decides for him.

Hypochondriac: A patient who can read the doctor's handwriting on the prescription.

I

Icicle: Eavesdropper.

Igloo: Icicle built for two.

Illegal: A sick bird.

Inlaws: The seeds in marriage that a man has to take along with the tomato.

J

Jam: What you get by eating forbidden fruit.

Jaywalking: The disease that could give you a rundown feeling.

K

Kangaroo: Texas grasshopper.

L

Lawyer Who Writes Wills: Heir-splitter.

M

Marital Squabble: When two people who have embarked on the sea of matrimony sail into each other.

Marriage: An institution held together by two books — cook and check.

Marriage: Where youth learns that love is an ocean of emotions surrounded by expanses of expenses.

Marriage License: Hunting permit that limits a girl's catch to one dear.

Marriage Where Wife Stays Home: A ways and means committee. She directs the ways. He provides the means.

Mental Block: Street on which ten psychiatrists and five psychologists live.

Middle Age: When the balance on the scales is no longer in your favor.

Miser: A man who lets the rest of the world go buy.

Modern Economy: Wall-to-wall carpeting and back-to-wall financing.

Money: It's called cold cash because in this economy a person can't keep it long enough to warm it up.

Moth Ball: What moths have in a closet full of wool suits.

N

Nervous: In a hurry all over.

Next-door Neighbors: Couple who hear both sides of your argument.

Nursery: Bawlroom.

O

Old Days: When stores advertised women's bathing suits as half off and meant the price.

Old Paint: A new shaving lotion for cowboys with a horsey smell.

Oldtimer: One who remembers when people counted blessings instead of calories.

Oldtimer: Grandfather clock.

Optimist: A mother who believes her daughter when she says, "It'll take only a minute for me to call Susie."

Optimist: A suburbanite who thinks the birds in his cherry tree are eating the worms.

P

Parachute: Air Force suspenders.

Pawnbroker: A merchant who lives off the flat of the land.

Pedestrians: The quick or the dead.

Pessimist: A man who grows his own crab grass.

Philosopher: A fellow who always knows what to do until it happens to him.

Pin-up Girl: One who won't sew on a button, so long as she can find a pin.

Politician: A man who says what he thinks, without thinking.

Politics: The art of talking more and saying less.

Pretzel Maker: Someone who gets rich by making crooked dough.

Psychiatrist: A man who advertises "consultation on a mania-back guarantee."

Public Relations Director: Praise agent.

R

Reckless Driver: any other motorist besides yourself.

Reincarnation: Five p.m. in an office when the boss sees his employees come back to life.

Relativity: The disease you have when your mother-in-law comes for two weeks and stays for ten.

Reindeer: Skinny animal with a TV antenna.

Resort: A place where you get a change and a rest. The waiters take your change and the motel takes the rest.

Responsibility: What one suspender button has when the other comes off.

S

Sophisticated Senior Citizen: Someone who can listen to the "William Tell Overture" without thinking, "Hi-Ho Silver, Away!"

Sourpuss: A cat in a lemon bin.

DAFFYNITIONS

Space Boss: Sir Launchalot.

Spring: The time when a young man's fancy turns to what the girls have been thinking about all winter.

Stage: What many a teenager girl thinks she should be on, when actually it's something she's going through.

Suburbia: A place where trees grow on money.

Suburbia: Where the houses are further apart and the payments are closer together.

T

Taxation: Modern method of spring cleaning.

Taxpayer's Anthem: "My Country, 'tis Not Free."

Teenager: Someone who will be complaining about the next generation.

Teenager's Cow: Four-legged milkshake.

Traffic Snarl: Three men pushing carts down the aisle of a supermarket.

U

Ulcers: What you get from mountain climbing over molehills.

Undercover agent: Insurance man in bed.

Undertaker: The last person to let you down.

Unlucky Man: He bent over to pick a four-leaf clover and a snake bit him.

Urban Necessities: A kerosene lamp for power failures. A horse for transit workers' strikes. A goat for garbage collectors' strikes.

V

Violin: A gift that has strings attached.

W

Wallpaper Store: A store where a wife buys and hangs the consequences.

Weather Bureau: Non-prophet agency.

Wedding: Where the bride looks stunning and the groom looks stunned.

Week End Alcoholic: He starts drinking on Tuesday and the week ends there.

Well-informed Man: His views are the same as yours.

Wheeler Dealer: Bike salesman.

Winter Weather Warning: Watch out for that freezy skid stuff. It can turn you into a slick stiff.

Wise Husband: One who buys his wife such fine china that she won't trust him to wash the dishes.

Woodpecker: The only creature that gets anywhere by knocking, and usually he ends up in a hole.

Worry: Today's mouse tasting tomorrow's cheese.

Y

Youthful Figure: What you get when you ask a middle-aged woman her age.

More Country Classics
Please send me...

Way Back in the Ozarks, by Howard Jean Hefley & James C. Hefley. Hilarious, heartwarming true stories of a boy named "Monk," his dog & his coon.

_____ Copies at $5.95 = _____

Way Back in the Ozarks, Book 2 by Howard Jean Hefley & James C. Hefley. "Ozark Monk" relives the tale of Danny Boy.

_____ Copies at $5.95= _____

Way Back in the Ozarks, VHS VIDEO TAPE. Meet "Ozark Monk" as he entertains you with stories from his first book. Filmed on location.

_____ Tapes at $15.95 = _____

Country Music Comin' Home, by James C. Hefley. Read about the stars, their triumphs and their tragedies, and how Christ is working in the country music industry.

_____ Copies at $5.95= _____

Ozark Mountain Hymns, Audio Cassette Tape features banjo, fiddle, dobro, mandolin & acoustic guitar. New songs & old time favorites.

_____ Tapes at $6.95 = _____

Please add $2.00 postage and handling for first book, plus $.50 for each additional book.

Shipping & Handling _____

MO residents add 6.7% sales tax _____

TOTAL ENCLOSED _____

Name_____

Address_____

City _____ State ___ Zip _____

Mail coupon with check or money order to: HANNIBAL BOOKS
921 Center
Hannibal, MO 63401

Call 800-747-0738 for quantity prices.